MOROCCAN MUSINGS

Groves of date palms along Morocco's Tafilalt and Drâa Valleys.
Photo: author.

Moroccan Musings

Anne B. Barriault

Drawings by Shawna Spangler

To order additional copies of this book, contact:
Xlibris Corporation
1-888-795-4274
www.Xlibris.com
Orders@Xlibris.com
97618

For Wanda, Barry, and Greer

CONTENTS

"Make baskets of your own," he would say, "make them all kinds of shapes and colors. But never forget that your baskets are made of something that is there for anyone to cut and use. And never imagine that you created the reeds yourself. You are only the person who shapes them into something that can be of use to others."

—Tahir Shah, *In Arabian Nights: A Caravan of Moroccan Dreams*

Preface and Acknowledgments

This little book was born of wanderlust, curiosity, ignorance, yearning, and desperation. What began as a quest for experience grew into remarkable relationships with others who are acknowledged in these pages. I have changed some of the names to protect the privacy of new friends who have enriched my life and inspired this book. My gratitude cannot possibly repay their kindness.

My interest in the Middle East gained urgency after the events of 9/11. One of the first things I said to a colleague after we watched the second tower fall was that we needed to better understand Islam and the multiverse that is the Muslim world. My own personal mission was to begin an education that might help to dispel the ignorance that existed within my own small universe.

Rereading these accounts, I am aware that my personal Moroccan discoveries started when I was struck by stars and consumed by desert fever. While this state has not exactly subsided, it has settled and, I hope, matured. The experiences that life presents lead to ever-evolving perspectives. But bear with me when I celebrate seemingly magical thinking in these pages. There is plenty of gritty despair on earth to temper these indulgences.

Poetic license aside, my Moroccan encounters have opened what I hope will be a continuing path of revelations. Just as the prose in these pages is often merely suggestive, so the art simply washes hints of the mysteries of people and places into view. Shawna Spangler's perceptive sensibilities and artistic hand more than transformed photographic images into evocative and imaginative works of art. I was honored that she was willing to work with me.

For the making of this book, I thank Sandy, Abdel, Adil, Kay, Betsy, Salwa, Paul, Sally, Daphne, Ruth, Jeri, the Xlibris team and my friends, family, and teachers in this and other countries. There are many variations for classic and Moroccan Arabic transliterations. While those in this text are imperfect at best, we have tried to be consistent, often choosing second spellings with roots in Berber and Arabic, those common in British publications, and those modeled in the books included in the select bibliography.

Finally, heartfelt thanks go to Randall Henniker, my husband and partner, for his encouragement, for wrestling with text and images with me, and for understanding my *djinns* better than I do.

PART 1

Imperial Cities and Other Sights

Kan, ya ma kan, Once there was and there was not.

—Laila Lalami, *Hope and Other Dangerous Pursuits*

PROLOGUE

There had been no miracle . . . Still . . . She wondered if there was
some other miracle she'd missed because she wasn't paying attention.
—Laila Lalami, *Hope and Other Dangerous Pursuits*

These Moroccan stories began in Sicily. My beloved villa group, who gather
every other year in Italy, had reunited once again in May, this time in the
northwestern part of an island that is a country unto itself and the crossroads of
ancient Mediterranean peoples. The villa that we rented was located outside of
Alcamo, home to Arab-Islamic cultures in the thirteenth and fourteenth centuries.
The influence is still present in the city's architecture. Occasional motifs—sensuous
domes and pointed arches, stone chevron patterns, tile and filigree—speak of
a mideastern and northern African heritage. Further south along the western
Sicilian coast, town walls bear modern, quickly scrawled Arabic graffiti betraying
vestiges of a lovely, ageless calligraphic alphabet. Medieval cathedral mosaics and
reliefs tell the tales of the Norman conquest over Islamic inhabitants, but traces of
that earlier civilization remain.

I found myself seeking Sicily's Arab-African heritage, urged by Sicilian winds
that grew into full-blown storms brought by the sirocco of the Sahara. I embraced
each coastal village that offered promises of glimpsing Africa with binoculars
on a clear day. I studied each Roman ruin with mosaic floors made of stone,
imported as displays of wealth from the African continent across the sea. By the
time we arrived in Mazara del Vallo, a town that has seen Phoenician and Greek
colonization, followed by Carthaginian, Roman, and then Arab, my fate was sealed.
Tunisian immigrants inhabit the Arab quarter there, where draped women stroll
among shops labeled in Arabic script.

The town of Erice was next to captivate me. Built atop a mountain dominating
the northwest coast of Sicily and dedicated to the ancient predecessor of the
goddess Venus, Erice is a medieval complex of tiny pedestrian streets and cold

stone churches. Clouds—called the veil of Venus—often envelop the town, soaking the unprepared tourist. Erice bears the mysteries of indigenous Sicilian societies, quietly attesting to a cultural mix of prehistoric, pagan, Christian, and Islamic traditions. It bewitched me so that I bought a tiny rug made locally of Arab-African design and colors whose meaning I would only discover later—indigo blue, saffron yellow, pomegranate red, and mint green. It was the closest that I thought I would ever come to northern Africa.

Then I met Samia, a Tunisian journalist, on my flight home from Palermo. We were seated together. She had just left her four-year-old son and his father behind to travel to the United States for the first time. We communicated through tears that turned to laughter. She spoke French by nature and a bit of English and was to attend a conference on American politics in Washington, DC, delivered in Arabic. She carried a beautiful book of ancient mosaics from Roman villas in Tunisia. As we marveled over its pages—stumbling through our pidgin French, Italian, and English—she suddenly offered the book to me, a present for the first person she met on her journey. I was touched by her kindness, as she apparently was by mine, though I insisted that she keep the book and await just the right moment to bestow it upon someone else whom she would later encounter on her trip. The art had already worked its magic on me. Northern Africa had beckoned on that Sicilian trip, and Samia reinforced it. The very next spring, the possibility of Morocco presented itself.

As my brother counseled, Africa gets into your blood. Stepping off the plane in Casablanca, I found the air pungent, acrid, and sweet, unmistakable and unlike the scents of Italy that had become so dear to me. African associations immediately imprinted themselves on my being. I was greeted by palm trees, humid breezes, and people with eyes of brown and amber, blue-green and gray, and complexions the color of coffee stirred with varying intensities of cream or cream tinted by various degrees of coffee. Morocco is home to the "grazing land" of Marrakech, the valleys of roses and date palms, deep gorges, snow-covered mountains, nomadic shepherds, and a countryside checkered by hedges built from prickly pear, rocks, or roses. The hotels are permeated with scents of orange and rose oils; the markets with mounds of olives, lemons, cinnamon, and turmeric—a crowded paradise kept in balance by life's suffering: the smell of blood from the butcher shops, beggars with shriveled limbs, and shops displaying live reptiles and pelts of exotic animals for ritual protection. *Inshallah.* As God wills, it is written.

Morocco—sensuous, intoxicating, spiritual, and earthbound. Samia understood as I recounted my reactions by e-mail when I returned home. Algeria had separated us on this trip, and though I could see its borders at one point along the journey, we could not see each other as we had hoped. Still, she understood as I confessed that I had found reasons for god and madness in a vast desert shot pink at sunrise and sunset.

Completely unbidden and unexpected, my experience was truly a "Moroccan discovery." That was the title of the museum excursion that I was fortunate to join. *Corny*, I thought, until its revelations made the aptness clear. Tourism at its very best, orchestrated by professional teams, the trip to Morocco's imperial cities was completely guided and controlled at every turn. Veiled, however, much like the country itself, were the surprises that filled so many beautifully bewildering moments. While skeptics may argue otherwise, Morocco assured me of a faith that miracles do happen around us as we live each day, though we are too blindly busy to see. Samia herself is of Berber descent, her grandparents immigrating to Tunis from the Atlas Mountains, home to Morocco's indigenous people. We believe that we met because we share sensibilities, trying to notice the daily lessons that present themselves over and over for us to learn and relearn. Stop, pay attention, listen, absorb, feel, and be. It is that simple. My personal discoveries, recounted in these pages, started with a starstruck case of desert fever that time has tempered into evolving perspectives on life as it presents itself.

For Samia and Sicily; for my husband, family, and villa travelers who love me enough to let me go; and for my Moroccan friends who made the trip with me, these vignettes are for each and every one of you with thanks.

THE SIROCCO AND THE MIRAGE

The North African wind gathers up dust, blowing violently from the south across the sea and mountains to islands and villages many kilometers away. In Sicily, the wind awakens you at 4:00 a.m. even before the shutters start rattling as it gains force, even before the doors slam shut, even before you rise to hook the windows and glance across the courtyard, watching trash as it spins into whirlwinds that skip across the pavement, scattering garbage to the corners. You marvel in disbelief as the wind catches in its path a tiny intruding country dog, helplessly levitated above the stones, paws scraping across the rocks and hopes dashed for a dinner of tossed-out leftovers. Sirocco.

The next year the winds carry me to Africa. Through the dust kicked up by gusts of wind, our drivers race each other in their tourist-teeming Land Rovers to the gateway of the Moroccan Sahara. Eventually, the dunes where the African gales originate loom before us. The landscape stretches endlessly. Gray-green brush turns to light-brown dirt as it reaches toward gentle hills of golden sand. Far on the desert horizon, a shimmer catches your eye—there, just before the rise, something mercurial on the surface of the grit, wet, reflective, and alluring. "Look, mirage," says our indifferent driver. It happens. He has seen it countless times before. We, his passengers, find it a wonder. To him, it is a daily phenomenon.

He delivers us up to sweet, uncomplaining camels on this particular day. They obligingly rumble and bumble us along the dunes and will return us to him when evening falls and their stomachs growl, ready to be fed.

As the sun begins to set, the sands change color again from a light mocha to a deep pink. Then magically, the dunes morph into a rich cinnamon. And we are mesmerized, watching tiny tornadic spouts sweep across the plain between the abundant curves of these soft-red dunes, stretching before us like spicy odalisques. The sands unfold uninterrupted before us. The sensual shapes and uniform texture make it impossible to gauge the vastness. But I know the winds are gathering there and eventually heading somewhere north to wake someone in a stormy Sicilian courtyard, as night falls fast in the desert, air chills, sand and sky blacken into one seamless continuum, and stars appear.

STORKS

Moroccan storks breed on haunted grounds. From their nests in Chellah, they overlook centuries-old decaying city walls; abandoned shrines, minarets, mosques, and schools long closed; and ancient Roman cemeteries overtaken by timeless cycles of weeds and wild flowers. Chellah is a sacred place for the dead and the living, built on a hill affording beautiful views of the valley. Here, flocks of bright-white ibis, with fuzzy orange crests, fill tall trees with deafening cries as though presiding over all the spirits who have walked or been laid to rest below. Between the commotion in the treetops and the utter stillness on the ground, the ancient ancestors make their hallowed presence known.

Sacred eels slither in a nearby pool of green water, caked by algae and tended by the keeper of feral cats, thin and hungry, hoping to warm their matted fur and tired bones in the sun when it finally breaks through the clouds. We are told that women wishing to conceive bring eggs to the eels on holy days. Except for the incessant chattering of birds, Chellah's eerie silence is disrupted at those times, filled by the voices of hopeful couples and their families. If their gift is accepted and consumed, it is a good sign for life. On this desolate day, however, overcast and gray with shadows of rain, Chellah is a bleak, forgotten, ghostly place, the heavy atmosphere thick with vapors of the past, not beings of the future.

The storks have seen it all. Paired in lonely couples, they fill their nests with twigs and perch to tend to their young, ignoring us. The huge birds glide through the air, and as they bend their spindly legs to land, they use their thin long beaks and enormous wings as instruments to guide their awkward bodies gracefully into their nests.

Located outside Rabat, Morocco's capital city, Chellah is surrounded by fourteenth-century walls that have witnessed the rise and fall of powerful dynasties. A huge stone gateway flanked by two towers marks the entrance, built by the Almohad and inscribed 1339. The following century saw the Merinid, who established the necropolis there for their loved ones. They built the tombs,

19

the mosque, and the theological school that served male students in their holy study. They left behind an ablution pool for purification and redemption and tiny cells for endless solitary recitations of the Koran. The Islamic scholars were later followed by the modern French, but long before them—among the ageless Berbers, Jews, and Arabs—the ancient Romans had conquered this place. A headless torso of a draped goddess stands guard over tombstones inscribed in Latin next to fallen shop stalls—all that is left of the ruined city of Sala Colonia.

At Chellah, rivulets have formed gorges, recording errant floods and descending to the deserted schoolyard. Though on this day, green with acanthus leaves reaching up to us as we pass by, the earth is also cracked, showing signs of parched suffering, brown and dry from centuries of drought, a microcosm of Moroccan extremes.

Meanwhile, the eels swim on, the cats and keeper quietly look to us for mercy, and the ibis flutter and squawk. The regal, silent storks, oblivious and triumphant, stand guard over this space of souls departed, this sacred place of prayers for life.

JANIE

If you really believe, a world of incredible possibility opens up, like the stairs in the "Tale of Mushkil Gusha" . . . But you must have the courage to climb.

—Tahir Shah, *In Arabian Nights: A Caravan of Moroccan Dreams*

The bus from Rabat to the holy cities of Meknes and Fes passes through an enchanted land. Beyond the king's equestrian grounds on the outskirts of the capital city, where groomsmen exercise noble stallions in fenced green pastures, the road becomes a pathway to the unexpected. You journey through silver olive groves to dark-green orchards of cork trees. Then suddenly you are in a land of white truffles, little mud-wrapped bundles of precious, flavorful fungi rooted by pigs in some countries, but here by dogs. You cannot see their vendors unless the bus stops. They emerge from nowhere. "They hide behind the trees," says our guide. "They are very thin." We laugh, uneasy, however, because of the utter strangeness of this trip still in its early stage. Little did we know that our eyes would prove him right when he teased that apes hide in the snow-covered cedars of the mid-Atlas range, wild boars snuffle along the rocky farmlands toward Marrakech, and grazing goats stand on their hind legs to reach tree leaves along the road from the holy city of Moulay Idriss. Before 2500 BCE, an ancient Mesopotamian sculptor fashioned an exquisite goat of wood, gold, and lapis lazuli that stands upright to reach a thin gold-leaf tree. The figure, small at twenty inches but of mythic proportions in our imaginations, finds a living counterpart in audacious Moroccan herds.

The land beyond the cork and olive groves turns rocky and reddish-brown. We pass single-story clay homes that could date to any bygone era. Except for the occasional satellite dish, these cottages are entirely ecological. The walls must be repaired after every rain, and if abandoned, they decay back into earth.

21

We glance and photograph, quickly but intrusively, tiny homes where a solitary toddler wanders outdoors, laundry hangs on a line, and buckets stand ready to collect water. Donkeys lumber along, carrying produce from the unusually fertile ground, graced this season by atypical amounts of rain. Mosques appear now and then to remind us of the rituals of prayer and meditation. Storks nesting on top of minarets and cell towers attest to the adaptability of life.

To the right on a hillside through the trees stands a whitewashed mosque within a cemetery. A group gathers there, dressed in brightly colored *djellabas*—traditional robes with pointed hoods—in deep turquoise, bright pink, and yellow, trimmed and sparkling with elaborate embroidery. Families have formed a funeral party to bury a loved one in a wooden casket marked, if wealthy, by a white tombstone, but just as often by a rock. The dead are laid to rest with their heads facing east toward Mecca in the Islamic tradition or—according to a seemingly unrelated Irish custom many miles and cultures away—toward the rising sun. I later learn that the mysterious indigenous Berbers of North Africa, who have kept their traditions despite conversions to Judaism or Islam, may have had connections to the ancient Celts, evolving into two green-eyed civilizations looking eastward.

Today on the bus, I am recording what I see as fast as I can in a leather-bound journal that my husband insisted I take on this trip. I thought it might be extra baggage but returned with its pages filled in gratitude. As I write this morning, my thoughts turn to Janie, his mother. She insisted that I go to Morocco, despite the fact that she was preparing for her final most adventurous journey, having withstood the agony of a terminal illness, determined to see it through its last phases without medical interference. As she slept, I kissed her on the head and offered a prayer—a blessing to protect her—the last time I saw her just days before I climbed aboard the plane. She was in the good hands of her devoted family and hospice nurses. After weekends of climbing into bed with her for naps that turned into hours of girl talk about our lives, I could do no more for her.

But today . . . today, she was here. While I wrote, her presence was palpable. A magnetic force is the only way I can describe it, compelling me to scribble poems and prayers to her, laced with desperate attempts to share with her what I saw outside the window as I crossed the Moroccan countryside—the ceremonies, the people, the poverty, the land. She was there, and she was not. But something electric, charged and larger than our lives on two continents, had me in its grip. So odd it was, so unlike anything I have ever experienced, and so unsolicited among the dark foliage and furtive glimpses into the private lives of rural Moroccans, that I noted the time, fully aware that something was happening to Janie's life and to mine.

That night when the phone rang in the hotel room, I knew even before I heard our guide's kind voice asking me to call my husband. "I know," I said, "it's Janie." When I returned my husband's phone call, I completed his sentence before he could even begin to tell me that Janie had died at 6:15 that morning. I will never be convinced otherwise that as she was gathering her energies to die, she had reached me on that bewitching road to the most holy city of Fes. It was as though in those early morning hours—late morning in Morocco—universal particles were stirring and drawing us together. That night, I realized that she had both found and left me in a good place, the muezzins calling us to prayer in the darkness after sunset and before dawn. As my friend said, Janie had kissed me good-bye, among the cork trees, white truffles, spirited cemetery, and lonely storks in flight along our travels.

"Put your hand over your heart for me in the desert." That was all that she had asked of me on my trip. The hour of her noonday funeral turned out to be the very hour of sunset on the dunes. As it happened, a short camel trek had been scheduled that day to take us to the Sahara for meditation or desert sledding, depending on your nature. I was able to place my hand over my heart for Janie late that afternoon, just when—though unknown to me at the time—her sons and great-grandson were speaking to friends and family gathered at her Virginia graveside and just before the western light from the Moroccan sun turned the sand to cinnamon, and the fireball sank behind the sands, giving over the day to the moonlit night.

HAREM, HAJBA, AND HANAN

> Life upstairs was so much easier, especially when everything was also
> accompanied by *hanan*, a Moroccan emotional quality that I rarely have
> encountered elsewhere . . . *Hanan* is hard to define exactly, but basically it
> is a free-flowing, easygoing, unconditionally available tenderness. People
> who give *hanan*, like Aunt Habiba, never threaten to withdraw their love
> when you commit some unintentional minor or even major infraction.
>
> —Fatima Mernissi, *Dreams of Trespass:*
> *Tales of a Harem Girlhood*

Author Fatima Mernissi observed *hanan* in certain family members of the
harem in which she grew up. Our guide explained from his heart, with *hanan,*
the concepts of a harem and *hajba*: the first, a man's means to gather the women
who are special to him or his obligations—wives, daughters, sisters, mothers,
mothers-in-law, divorced or widowed aunts—together in a place that offers
protection and sanctuary; the second, a condition of marriage whereby the woman
never leaves the house over which she has complete dominion. While she was not
part of a harem, our guide's own mother exemplified *hajba*; although after having
married at age twelve to become the widowed mother of sixteen children, she
finally left her house in 1972. She regretted leaving, he told us.

Her youngest child, now our protector and guide, became a representative
of his culture, an impassioned and dispassionate interpreter at once. He led us
deep into *medinas* along the stucco facades of centuries-old Moroccan homes
surviving to this day in the medieval sections of each city. An occasional window
covered by elaborate iron grillwork high above us would catch our eye and trigger
speculation—veiled windows allowing light into interiors and views onto the
street. Some in our group saw them as locked to any possibility for the women
of the households—whether harem or *hajba*—to escape or even leap to suicide,

as one observer dryly noted. Perhaps true, but perhaps a Western misguided perception—a mirage for which we might hope to receive *hanan*.

Having grown up in the feminist age in academics, I nevertheless have often empathized as I've read accounts by medieval Italian merchants ruminating about the fates of their daughters. Worried sick about their children's futures, fathers of girls would set aside money for dowries to pay for marriage or the convent to guarantee survival, intended out of love or obligation rather than a desire to imprison or restrict, although these social realities morphed into suppression. I would have been a concerned Italian father too, but I also would have been a restless Moroccan daughter trying to pry off the interlaced grillwork of windows that kept me from the outside world.

The modest Moroccan sensibility hides, protects, and veils good fortune from external jealousies. Compliments are uninvited and not easily accepted. Wealth is a private matter, guarded behind decaying walls. Medallions of the hand of Fatima, the Prophet's daughter, decorate every other door to protect against the evil eye. Beneath traditional women's *hijabs* and *djellabas*—scarves and robes—are centuries of beauty and love potions, gold jewelry, hennaed hair, and elaborate drapery, disguised and hidden from public display.

Imagine what tourism does to such a private culture revealed earnestly with pride by guides seeking to educate but often inviting unwelcome attention that many would want to divert. What seems to be a genuinely tender Moroccan sense of courtesy and a desire not to disappoint—about which much has been written—sometimes gets scrambled when a more extroverted culture views a more introverted one, causing a collision of expectations and assumptions.

Moroccan modesty and *hanan*, even the harem and *hajba*, are quite the opposite of ancient Greek hubris, guaranteed to cause painful lessons when human perceptions of superiority are flagrantly displayed to challenge the gods. The colossal Greek temples in Sicily, the great feats of architecture erected to please the gods, may express the latter condition; the dilapidated houses in Morocco the former.

Unremarkable describes the exterior of Moroccan houses. But cross the threshold if you are lucky to be invited in, and everything changes. Marble floors cool your feet, colorful tiled walls dazzle your eyes as far you can see, bright silk and brocade fabrics invite you to recline on the cushioned banquettes, and white, lacelike plaster filigree decorates each curving arch, pillar, and planed surface above you, lifting your spirits with it as it ascends to the skylight. Calligraphic Koranic blessings carved at eye level offer prayers for good fortune, for Allah to provide.

Impoverished homes outnumber houses of great luxury, of course. From the street, you might catch an unsolicited glimpse into ordinary family life behind a cracked door. Children inside a tiny courtyard play on dirt floors, watered and swept by their mothers and aunts in daily battles against the elements. There are no chairs in sight. One woman eyes you with suspicion, but another smiles warmly and knowingly. You smile back. Fated or not, chosen or not, this is home and a private affair.

My mentor laughs to this day as he recounts a meeting long ago when he had tried to convince me to leave the field, despairing that there were no jobs in a world outside the harem of graduate school. I informed him that I would not give up but would have to make my living regardless, and although I was married, I would never be a kept woman. Working paycheck by paycheck every year afterward to tend to my own private life and fated home, how often have I wondered what it would have been like to choose, or rather to have had chosen for me, life in a harem as a housewife or concubine.

Moroccan concubines, we are told in Marrakech, were selected for their beauty and talents by their local villages as gifts to the viziers—the prime ministers in power—in exchange for political safeguards. In one palace, the women's apartments open onto an inner courtyard. They worked out their lives among themselves, their children, and the vizier's wives and families, located in another part of the complex. They would remain with the house after the vizier fell from grace, when another man would replace him.

In her large photographs of contemporary veiled Moroccan women, artist Lalla Essaydi transforms the ninth-century harem practice of *washi*—erotic poetry and messages written on thin fabric by women to attract and undermine men—into personal expressions of feminist thinking. Said to originate in Baghdad (though some trace it to Japan), *washi* communicated poetic messages and promises of love inscribed on handkerchiefs and headbands to upset the balance of domestic power. A beautiful, mysterious calligraphic hand covers the fabrics in which Essaydi drapes her subjects, decorates their faces, and fills the background settings of her photographs. Called a "digital Scheherazade" by writer Fatima Mernissi, Essaydi entices the viewer with her delicate, intricately patterned imagery while conveying a powerful message: I am not here for your entertainment; I am not your property. Her images comprise an unsettling subtlety and disarming directness simultaneously as her subjects emerge from their settings to lock eyes with the viewer or completely turn their backs on those who look.

Essaydi's art attempts to capture childhood memories of Marrakech, she says. In one polyptych, she traces the evolution from girlhood to womanhood. Each stage is embodied by a progressively more draped and hidden female model: a loose-haired young girl in a delicate tunic, a preteen donning a *hijab*, a young woman veiled to reveal only her eyes, a mature woman swallowed up by a *burka* and entirely hidden from view. As sexuality becomes more potent, so the drapery to deny or acknowledge, disguise or conceal, protect or claim it grows more abundant.

"Who doesn't want to be a concubine?" I ask my group of sister and fellow travelers standing within the herb- and floral-scented courtyard of the concubines' quarters. No one laughs. Job security, yes, but high stakes. Your mission was to serve as a silent, inside village presence in the palace, strategically placed to witness and report home, only to risk the vizier's displeasure and the possibility of being discovered and discarded, especially in old age. You are given sanctuary in a harem only to face exile without one.

"The sultan had 24 wives and 200 *porcupines*," writes a nine-year-old in an essay shared by a teacher on the trip with us. *But life as a porcupine may be more common than we imagine,* I ponder as I scan the faces of the wives and husbands with whom I am touring—the ones who did not laugh. I think about the demands of our own social expectations and conventions. I wonder about our hard-earned but conspicuous displays of achievement and wealth—jewelry, clothing, homes—that veil the realities of our domestic and working lives, our often *hajba*-like assignments. I contemplate the compromises that we all have to make to survive. We place lovely grilled windows over our hearts and sometimes around those we jealously love, showing others only occasional guarded glimpses of our spiritual interiors. Hubris and *hanan*, arrogance and tenderness, may be two sides of a coin.

THE BOYS

Moroccan children are winsome and beautiful. Friendly and curious, they greet you wherever you go. Hoping for candy but asking for a *stilo,* they happily accept pens, stickers, or chocolate. They always request something more for their younger siblings, who stand shyly at a distance at first. If you begin to proffer little gifts, however, the children flock like birds competing for your attention. If left helpless without a guide in sight to rescue you, you can turn the chaos into lessons for good manners, if you are lucky. *Ecoutez, attendez, dite merci*—"listen, wait, say thank you"—you state with authority to mask your haplessness.

Jameel and Aloued—handsome gents of elementary school age—fell into step with me as we toured their *ksar* in Rissani. Their families live in this adobe fortress centered around a central well within the city gates. Just outside, drivers park their horse-drawn carts at an equine taxi stand, waiting to take veiled women to the market.

Endless dark corridors twist and turn in the cavernous setting of the *ksar,* revealing tiny doorways to protected homes. Children brandishing sticks, wheels, and rags meet to play at the corners of the passageways where sunlight falls; their mothers, aunts, and grandmothers step outside the doors of their domiciles as you pass by. Wary, weary, but welcoming, they nod hello.

My two new friends were dressed up that day. Hands in pockets, they nonchalantly chatted with me as we walked. We named the colors of their patterned sweaters; Jameel's in olive green, pale yellow, and gray; Aloued's in deep blue, purple, red, and green. We talked about how good school was. We counted to ten. We were speaking in French, Arabic, and English; they laughed at my errors, trying to help me improve my language skills. When our visit had ended, they escorted me to the bus and waited politely until we departed. I blew kisses through the window to them; they waved and grinned and kept my heart in exchange.

Seven- and eight-year olds grow to be twelve and thirteen. By that time, the boys are learning the sales trade. Traveling in small groups, they offer you pendants, euros, and little camels woven from the fronds of date palms. If an object is refused, an occasional teen will insist on making it a gift, only to return a while later awaiting compensation. The most meaningful mementos that I brought home were not the ceramics or the rugs, the scarves, or *kufi*—knit skullcaps—but two dried palm-leaf camels and one gazelle, as well as a fake fossil pendant purchased for $1.25. I wear it all the time and am astonished by the compliments. Its salesman was a young man in Erfoud, who was genuinely surprised that I could say "good morning" and count in Arabic, and he was delighted to claim that my new president was African. Barack Obama is a source of great pride on both sides of the Atlantic.

Another young vendor of palm-frond animals also liked the USA. I am guessing that he had seen little of the world outside the steep Todra Gorge in his fourteen years or so. After what had become my requisite recitation of Arabic numbers to entertain each new group of boy salesmen, I asked him in French, "Where do you live? Are you in school?" and told him how much I loved his beautiful country. He smiled broadly, answered, thanked me, and told me that he had a girlfriend in Ohio.

Earlier, a young attendant in the hotel shop had spoken with us about his family and his ambitions beyond postcard sales. He was going to college in the States the following year. I bought postcards, gave him my card, and told him where to find me; he handed me a small polished fossil. I held my breath, hoping that he would find his reception in our country to be as safe and warm as ours had been in his.

Later during a four-hour stretch through the Atlas Mountains, we stopped at a towering overlook along one of the thousands of curves in the road. I fell into conversation with a man in a bright-yellow tunic and turban who was making the same trip with a buddy in a sports car. He beamed when I told him that I lived near Washington, DC. He had studied at Georgetown and the University of Pennsylvania fifteen years ago. "I was a smart man then, but I ain't no more!" he exclaimed, encouraging me to study Moroccan Arabic and return to *his* country, a decision that the beauty of abundant pomegranate trees would make for me when I saw them, he assured me. *Where shall we be fifteen years from now?* I thought, wondering where the years would lead the young hotel-shop attendant, my newfound boy-salesmen friends, and my smart college man.

THE GIRLS

Young girls in traditional marketplaces stare at you. By the time they reach adolescence and the age to cover their heads with the *hijab*, the scarf that expresses religious commitment or simply a conservative upbringing, they are also assessing the cultural differences that surround them. As I purchased a camera battery or bottle of water from a shop-keeping father, his daughters would scrutinize my curly hair, my skin, my eyeglasses, my jacket. One young lady was riveted, and no matter how many Arabic parlor tricks I tried from my limited supply—*sabbah il kheer, tosha raffnah* (good morning, nice to meet you)—even stooping to counting to ten, she would not smile. She looked deeply into my eyes as though searching to find what I was made of.

Women in Morocco's major cities register the changes in society and the multiplex that is their country. My favorite sights in Marrakech, city of modern European boulevards and ancient snake charmers, are pairs of women—a driver and a passenger—draped head to toe, buzzing around town on motorbikes. Trios of women—three generations in one family—can often be seen walking together. The elders are completely covered by *hijabs* and *djellabas* of color and pattern that would be the envy of ancient Silk Road traders. Their daughters wear *djellabas* too, though just as often European pants, skirts, and jackets, topped by *hijabs* that reveal only their faces—beautiful eyebrows and eyes accented in kohl. The third generation—the granddaughters—have defied tradition, however, and are decked in the latest boots, tank tops, and miniskirts inspired by international pop stars.

On the Prophet's birthday, many townspeople dress up for the holiday, visiting one another with cakes and bread. Strolling around Marrakech, I passed a father with two children in a square. The toddler was adorned in traditional finery—tunic, pants, and fez of white silk embroidered in gold—turning every head as he wobbled around. In contrast, his older sister wore casual clothing. Tall and lanky, she might have been eleven and was completely unselfconscious in her bright-pink running suit. I walked by them and then turned to take a picture, an afterthought for which I should have asked permission. The image captures a perfect triangulation: the dad in a denim jacket and baseball cap is distracted, trying to keep up with his children; the little boy's attention is focused on something fascinating on the ground; but the girl flashes an engaging smile as she looks over her shoulder into my lens.

Girls and boys go to school together now in Morocco. Soccer is huge. Education is compulsory through age fifteen, and classic Arabic, French, and English are requisite. Today, female students outnumber their male counterparts at the University of Rabat. The king married a computer scientist and has done much to advance women's rights. Morocco has recently made a bold move to open the doors of theological study to women who desire to study the Koran and its interpretations to become imams.

While observations may be mirages, women share government positions with men, they teach in universities, and they run restaurants and private businesses. Many are professors, doctors, and lawyers, though many still produce traditional embroidery and pastry dough for the marketplaces. These *souks* are the province of men, however; salesmen run the shop stalls.

Yet unemployment is high. Young men gather along the streets and hover in alleys, and male storytellers circle together in ancient squares. Elder patriarchs sit in cafés throughout the day in urban and rural areas; men drink coffee in country bars, while women can be seen in nearby fields, gathering vegetables, herbs, and firewood.

I will always wonder whatever became of the woman who was the shining, shocking-pink girl in my photo of the marketplace. That bright, sunny morning was dedicated to the Prophet, and I shall think about what sort of promise that smiling girl was able to fulfill.

ARTFUL FORMS

"The Arabs were a desert people, and they found the emptiness frightening," Rachid told me . . . "Zellij is like a metaphysical science, used to make space measurable."

—Suzanna Clarke, *A House in Fez*

The fine art of calligraphy is deeply embedded in Islamic architecture. Sacred texts are carved in plaster within the walls of many a Moroccan holy place and upper-class home. The purity of sheer ornament overwhelms the interiors. Style and content are one—a message conveyed through its medium. Simple elegance turns hard surface into white lace. Artful forms—letter and pattern—completely transform spaces into visions of transporting serenity.

The Bahia Palace in Marrakech, the tomb of Moulay Ishmaïl in Meknes, Fes's mosques of Fatima and Miriam and its House of Music, and Casablanca's great mosque of Hassan II all bear artisans' bas-reliefs conveying the holy word. Walls and archways sing of the spirit in beautiful prayer.

Bahia means "palace of the beautiful" or "the favorite." Two powerful prime ministers, a vizier and his son, built the complex in the nineteenth century. Si Moussa oversaw the creation of the older section in the palace; his son, Ba Ahmed, the newer one. Each section wraps around a central courtyard redolent with cypress, jasmine, herbs, banana plants, and orange trees. The palace was named for one of four beloved wives.

Father and son imported the best craftsmen and materials from across the Moroccan kingdom to decorate their home: cedar from middle Atlas mountains for the ceiling and doors, marble from the northern city of Meknes for the floor, and tiles for the walls from the city of Tétouan on the Mediterranean coast—known in medieval Arabic poetry as the "little Jerusalem," "the daughter of Granada," "the sister of Fes," and "the white dove."

Everywhere I looked, ornate floral patterns and precise geometric designs caught my eye and took my breath away. Dazzling art completely enveloped me in a domestic setting that evoked associations with Michelangelo's Sistine Chapel frescoes in a sacred space.

Encircling the columns and inlaid across pilasters and flat planes, colorful tiles create notes of point and counterpoint: green, the color of Islam; blue, the color of Fes; yellow, a Berber color; and white. Above, fields of intricate flowers cover the ceiling in painted cedar intarsia. The pigments are organic: green derives from mint, blue indigo from Asian plants, orange from the pomegranate, yellow from saffron, and red from poppies.

However, unlike Michelangelo's paintings—centered on the human figure and its relationship to the Christian divine—here, all images are ornamental, based purely on essence. The Vatican's setting is sacred; the one in Marrakech is secular, and yet Islamic architecture intertwines the two domains. Decoration carries the spiritual belief that soulful beings—divine, human, or animal—should not be physically represented.

The word is made visible, however, and it is written. At eye level, ornate plasterwork records sacred texts in a graceful calligraphic dance, morphing into pure interlace as patterns ascend over arches to the skylight. Interiors of palaces, mosques, theological schools, and large homes, called *riads*, are replete with such carving. A *riad* resembles an Italian Renaissance *palazzo* with origins in ancient Roman architecture—where life revolves around a central square courtyard—leading up to three or four floors of interior rooms opening onto balconies on all four interior sides. While the viziers' Bahia palace situated families in separate horizontal spaces—wives and their children in apartments around the first courtyard, concubines and their children around the second—*riads* housed the family vertically in the upper stories, a mother-in-law in one quarter, a wife and children in another, widowed or divorced aunts in a third, and men gathered around the ground-floor courtyard.

The House of Music is such a *riad*, located in the medieval section of Fes, the traditional Islamic seat of Morocco. The house had served families before its life as a European music conservatory in the early twentieth century. With time, the role of the house had changed from the center of Moroccan domestic life to the center of a French artistic one. Today, photographs of musicians, a European playbill, a violin bow, and pages of music preserve memories of the building's life as the House of Music, set against the serene rhythms of ancient Arab decor.

Walking to the House of Music through Fes's narrow corridors of stucco, clay-colored homes, we passed the shops of bakers, tailors, and metalworkers until we could wend our way down a shoulder-wide path too narrow for the city's pack mules and donkeys. Stepping into the house, I let the noisy chaos of the medina slip away while I stood mesmerized by an interior of breathtaking harmony and symmetry. The saying that music is fluid architecture and architecture is frozen music is manifested here.

A fountain stands as the courtyard's centerpiece while side columns reach several stories high to a skylight that once opened to the heavens. *Zellij*—the now-familiar geometric green, blue, yellow, and white tile—greets the visitor, and lacelike plasterwork surrounds graceful calligraphy before climbing the upper walls and crossing high archways.

Sometimes the writing, which advances from right to left, creating the silent, serene, and timeless beauty of the sacred word, is left in the pure-white state of the plaster; sometimes it is painted in a black glaze.

Artisans worked the letters of the flowing Arabic alphabet by hand in moist plaster, carving as much as could be accomplished in a day before it dried. As our guide explained, technical training is available in Morocco so that "if you cannot use your brain, you can use your hands." Any opportunity helps the battle for employment, and although modern plaster carving can be purchased from molds, the hand-carved ancient and modern calligraphy speaks of something more than just technical skills.

We read promises that "Allah will take care of you" as well as wishes for universal household blessings. In the courtyards and great rooms, gentle calligraphic carving offers prayers for "health, wealth, and luck," good fortune that any household in the world could certainly use.

The Kasbah

What is missing from these pages? The *kasbah* of course. Come with me.

Kasbah is defined originally as a medieval castle fortress built by a powerful family and harboring villagers within its bewildering passageways. Today the adobe ramparts, pathways, and doorways retain that majestic mirage though very real independent homeowners and squatters now inhabit the endless apartments locked within fortified walls. For Westerners, the word kasbah evokes images of Humphrey Bogart's *Casablanca*. Warner Brothers and Bugs Bunny implanted images of "kasbahs" in our consciousness. But what do we really know of them?

My introduction occurred on the bus to Rabat's kasbah the first night in Morocco. We were on our way to a consummate Moroccan dinner at an extravagant restaurant, when the guide informed us that it was located in the kasbah off the main avenue. Its narrow corridors prohibited vehicles from entering, and we would have to walk a bit to get there. We would also be inclined, unaware, to pass by this place of elegant dining—so nondescript was the exterior; so hidden were its riches.

The city's main avenue extends past gateways on the right to the University of Rabat, now a model for Arab colleges. A sign at that juncture indeed reads kasbah in French, Arabic, and English and points to the left. From the American tour bus, I caught the eye of two young men about to enter the university walls, both of whom began gesturing and mouthing to me, "Come with me to the kasbah," in a mocking impression of Charles Boyer. Despite my fatigue from the flight to Casablanca, the bus trip to Rabat, and a day figuring out the ratio of *dirhams* to dollars, I laughed out loud.

Medieval kasbahs, made of a mixture of clay and straw, were fortresses logically built on hills with meandering paths and secret passageways for defense. Enemies were sure to lose their way, defeated by the residents, whose peace the intruders wanted to disrupt. Charles Boyer's kasbah in the late-1930s film *Algiers* fueled Western perceptions of the mysterious Arab cultures that it sheltered—exotic, inaccessible, lawless, threatening, but irresistible. Gillo Pontecorvo's political film, *The Battle of Algiers,* contains a scene in which a desperate French official in the 1950s manages to plant a bomb that blows up a portion of the kasbah. The frames of contemporary destruction and timeless grieving villagers are chilling. We remember that hundreds of people died during anti-French protests in Algeria and Morocco in 1955 alone before the countries gained their independence.

"If you get lost in the medina or the kasbah, stay where you are—we will notice you are missing and backtrack to find you," our guides constantly cautioned us. The adage is not unlike that quoted by the Yorkshire poet David Whyte, "If you get lost in the forest, stand still. The trees are not lost." It is an old Native American proverb rekindled by the author in his efforts to reach those currently confused by the twists, turns, and blind alleys of modern life. We were experiencing the Arab-African version of the proverb, passed down to us from ancient cultures.

Rabat's kasbah, built under Andalusian influence in the twelfth century, has now become desirable real estate. Whitewashed walls are painted halfway up in a deep blue that matches the sky on a crystal clear day. Clay containers, also painted blue, house exotic trees and flowers outside the small doorways that lead to secretive, enclosed homes within the all-embracing complex. Very expensive, very fashionable, very popular with the Europeans, we were told. At night, the pathways are empty except for bands of young men hanging out. The days are filled with bustling activity balanced by the silence of what lies behind the doors, armed with amulets to stave off trouble. Steps away from the walled-in houses, though I could not retrace the path if I tried, an open-air café painted in the same blue and white offers café noir or mint tea to the residents and visitors who meander through the kasbah's mazelike corridors. A young armless man stood in the pathway leading to the café, beseeching me for alms.

His plight opened a window to darker tales told by kasbahs—one, the majestic fortress of Ait-Ben-Haddou that sits atop a gorge near Telouet. Terra-cotta-colored, it towers over the valley, accessible only by donkeys and their young drivers who ford the Imarene River that separates the kasbah from the town. They, like Charon, ferry their passengers across the water to visit the kasbah; we, like the newly dead, accepted the rides, emboldened by curiosity about our only half-realized predicament. The river that day was muddy from all the rain, the shores were muddy, the landscape was muddy, the architecture was muddy. The skies were heavy and low, laden with gray clouds. Delivered by burros to the kasbah's shore, we stood in awe, just before beginning the trek upward. There, on low ground, we beheld a huge arched entrance, the same mud-red color of the imposing kasbah that rose behind it. We imagined the medieval vizier who constructed the complex, only one of many exemplary structures along Morocco's magnificent route of one thousand kasbahs. Many sites had existed in the seventeenth and eighteenth centuries as cities unto themselves—slave and villager quarters at the base, the ruling family ensconced in the fort at the top. But the pasha of this kasbah turned out to be a member of the notorious Glaoui clan—a ruling French-partisan family during the early twentieth century who completed the fortress. Guests at such kasbahs included Winston Churchill and Colette.

In fact, during the 1950s as the Glaoui and the French capitulated to Moroccan nationalists, a French actress had made this kasbah her home. The impressive archway at its entrance, as it turns out, was constructed solely for late-twentieth-century movies. A plane flew through the arch in a recent film (*Jewel of the Nile, Gladiator, The Mummy, Kundun, Babel,* and *Sahara,* in fact, were all made in this region and nearby Ouarzazate, the center of the Moroccan movie industry).

Climbing the steep urban switchbacks that lead past the adobe apartments to the crown, we encountered impoverished young families with their babies. Squatters in camps that they call home within the kasbah's walls sell paintings, fabrics, herbs, and spices to tourists. Once in a while, we would spot other signs of life—a *tagine,* Morocco's conical terra-cotta cooking pot—sitting abandoned on an extinguished firebed or a donkey quietly grazing on a lunchtime sack of feed. Goats bleated from corrals built on the ancient skywalks and terraces above us as we traversed the narrow, mud-rutted footpaths to our destination. The higher we climbed, the fewer the inhabitants, the wider the view of the mountainous terrain that crested above the surrounding valley. The brown, barren earth unfolded before us like a forsaken moonscape. Certainly, approaching visitors, whether hostile or friendly, would be spotted from this height long before they actually arrived. The views of the sweeping mountains that rimmed the bleak plains more than compensated for our efforts to reach the pinnacle that afforded such sights. Elevated above the impoverished lives below us, several of us joked halfheartedly that we could stay here forever. Forever. Who would notice? Who would miss us? The Moroccan discovery had led us thus far to this abandoned, colorless spectacle, and Marrakech, teeming with seductive life and sunshine, was still ahead. But in efforts to escape whatever we perceived our personal plights to be, we were inviting one another not to come to the kasbah (Charles Boyer, as it turns out, never uttered that famous phrase to Hedy Lamarr in *Algiers*) but to remain here.

"If you get lost in the forest, stand still." Two of our group forgot to heed the guides' warning and had wandered off. As we slowly realized that our numbers were reduced by two and launched a search party for the disappeared, we were unaware that the donkeys and their drivers at the riverbank had also gone missing. Once our own abandoned fates gradually became clear, we realized that our path home would be wet but inevitable. Our entire group, minus the missing pair, hesitantly consented to wade back across the river to the bus through the rushing muddy waters, a practical decision that only fed our romantic desires to remain in the kasbah forever.

Shoes off, pants hiked up, cameras gingerly balanced, feet soaked cold as ice, and gritty up to our thighs—well, actually, only our calves—we all agreed later that this passage would be the best story of the trip. With each telling of the tale, the waters ran deeper, and the minnows morphed into leeches and crocodiles.

"*Elles sont disparue* and the burros as well," I lamely explained soon after the crossing to an amused Mustapha, our incomparable and always slightly bemused bus driver, as my soaked, mud-caked legs dried and my eyes scanned the area for missing passengers, donkeys, and French vocabulary. We eventually recovered everyone and everything except the *ânes*, the burros, and their boy attendants, who had not yet been paid for their services. We later found out that they had been ushered away by order of the town mayor, the present-day pasha who wanted to exert his power to clear the site for a newly arrived film crew.

After a While

Tourism is a burgeoning industry in Morocco. A network of people whose vast reaches often go unnoticed by travelers—Moroccan guides and bus drivers, roadside vendors and souk-keepers, hotel clerks and restaurant owners work together to carefully orchestrate tourist experiences. The welfare and happiness of their charges is the first priority in their kind and tireless, interconnected efforts to make a living.

In Rabat, Abdul joined our group to show us his capital city. "Everyone is named Abdul," said Abdel, the divine conductor of our entire Moroccan excursion. He also answered to "Abdul," reassuring us that by calling anyone Abdul, we would rarely get a name wrong. Rabat Abdul lectured about the king and parliament, grew impatient with our inattention, but bravely withstood angry voices from the food stalls protesting the tourists who traipsed through their markets and gawked.

Haj fell into step with us in the Fes marketplace. A man of small stature with a quiet but commanding voice, he helped to herd us through the crowded medina, counting his sheep, cautioning us about mud puddles, uneven steps, and low wooden beams. We were not at all sure who he was at first, and we assumed that he had simply attached himself at the rear of the group. As the days went by, however, we realized that he was instrumental to keeping our congregation together. His French and English appeared to be impeccable, his patience in listening to my first attempts to speak Arabic unmatched. He embodied the quality of *hanan*, gracious and compassionate.

Abdel excelled as our pied piper. Our multilingual shepherd, he rarely left our side, delivering us up to our hotels, arranging the meals, and connecting us to the assigned guides of each new territory. He offered countless personal courtesies, quietly observing and catering to every need or interest, no matter how large or small. He neglected no one. Barbara required a new watch to keep up with our schedule. Kathy's hands were frozen from the unexpected winter chill of the spring torrents and needed gloves. Frank had to find a pharmacy. Joslin had a passion for textiles. Eileen and Randy collected antiques. Adele and Judy jumped at the chance for a cooking class. Abdel kept our pastoral symphony in sync at all times.

In Fes, Abdel introduced us to Azid. Both handsome men—self-possessed with a balance of sternness tempered by tenderness and a subtle sense of the ridiculous—the two of them together worked in perfect harmony. They lectured, demonstrated, humored, and advised each of us on our stops at city gates and carpet centers, historic mosques, and theological schools. Their concert at House of Music was a perfect recital that set the tone of our trip. This breathtakingly beautiful *riad* had once been a private residence and then, under the French, a music school filled with European notes. Our guides presented the history of this building such that no architectural feature or aspect of human nature and family dynamics went unnoticed. The mothers-in-law's quarters were located upstairs on the opposite side of the courtyard from the wives' quarters, they drolly remarked.

Daily, Abdel and his troupe transported and overwhelmed their wards with cultural information, delivering us safe and exhausted to the hotel each evening. Security is an unspoken concern, with the goal to keep visitors undisturbed and unaware of undercover police and many cell phone calls invisibly made to and from authorities to protect Americans, Europeans, and Russians especially.

Our guides' attentiveness even extended to our encounters with merchants. Opportunities to purchase guidebooks or jewelry abounded as street vendors accosted wide-eyed visitors, making novices of even the most experienced and intrepid travelers among us. Arching a brow in an elegant shop, Azid whispered that we had chosen well but could do better as we bargained with an insistent carpet salesman. Abdel exchanged my newly purchased French guidebook for a more practical one in English and suggested that for the cost of my ceramics, the factory should give me a present. I chose a dainty eggcup for my sister-in-law.

From time to time, our shepherds allowed their flock to explore on our own so that we could practice our consumer skills. A young husband and father followed me around Rissani with necklaces displayed along his arm. "*S'il vous plaît, madame.* This necklace is onyx and silver, of Berber design and very beautiful." "*Vraiment?*" I asked politely but skeptically, as I kept walking. "Please, madame, I have two wives and four daughters." "*C'est vrai?*" I asked again. When I commented that he was surrounded by a lot of women in his household, he said it was not all bad. "In fact"—he smiled at me—"it is quite nice, and I am blessed." As I boarded the bus, I bought the necklace for less than $3. He was happy, and I was happy. I wear my silver-and-black Berber beads often, and each time, they conjure up visions of the vendor's household, whatever the true number, gender, or marital status of its inhabitants.

In contrast, our Land Rover driver who served us up to the camels was serious and reticent. He revealed his story only in the darkness surrounding our car after the trek, as I whispered to him in rusty French while he concentrated on following his headlights and the stars to search out our return paths from the desert. He was the eldest son of eight children, born to a Berber family who lived nearby. Three married sisters lived elsewhere; he and his four brothers stayed at home. When I asked, he softly translated the traditional Berber love song playing for us on the Land Rover's CD about a sorrowful woman without a husband.

In Marrakech, I encountered a far-from-sorrowful woman of boisterous independence, wearing a bright spring-green *hijab* and *djellaba* with *niqab*—a thin black veil covering her mouth and nose. It revealed her smiling eyes. Busy ambushing travelers with her wares, she was unusual—first for being a female vendor, second for her happy aggression, and third for her attire. When it finally became clear that I was not going to buy her multiple silver bracelets, she lightly pinched me on the arm and said, "See you later, alligator. After a while, crocodile." She laughed as she got the surprised reaction that she had anticipated. Later, when I asked Abdel about her, he told me that she acts and dresses in an irritating manner for tourists.

Then there was Said, "Bond, James Bond, Morocco," as he introduced himself, though our group soon came to know him as Shake-a-Leg. "Shake-a-Leg" was his herding cry, a command that kept us moving. Helping to lead us through the bustling, bewildering Marrakech medina, ensuring that no one got lost or left behind, he would also occasionally drive his senior female charges with the imperative "Let's go, mother!" He would regularly chant "Yalla, yalla! [Let's go!]" It became the group cheer, and I hear myself saying it to my dogs now. They also respond to "Oushe," the camel drivers' hushed word used to persuade the beasts to settle down and sit still.

We obeyed our commands. We had been told to wear scarves to protect ourselves from windblown sand while on our little Saharan trek. To our surprise, the camel drivers then fashioned these scarves into elaborate turbans—*cheches*—on the heads of select female explorers to complete their mini Lawrence-of-Arabia experience. Our group of independent world-travelers had actually been well-trained, and we delighted to hand ourselves over willingly to such artful orchestrations, humorous with just enough of a "Shake-a-Leg" edge to keep us in line, but not without that touch of tenderness too.

EPILOGUE

Look into the eyes of a Jinn, and stare into the depths of your soul.
—Tahir Shah, *The Caliph's House*

Spiritual counterparts, advisers, and troublemakers, *jinns* or *djinns* (sprites or genies) are believed to have been created of fire after Allah made human beings of clay. They appear in the Koran. It is said that djinns, angels, and human beings share the highest intelligence of all creatures. The Moroccan belief in djinns' existence and in their seriously wicked antics, taunting and tormenting all that is human, fill many a page scripted by travel writers and expatriates who have lived in that country. In Morocco, djinns most certainly have a clever way of mirroring human behavior and taking the blame, as acknowledged in the Moroccan proverb quoted by author Tahir Shah. Traditional Moroccan stories, after all, begin by saying, "Once there was and there was not."

I wrote this book because Moroccan djinns followed me home. They got into my brain, my heart, my soul, and my computer. Though mythology tells us that the human and the djinn worlds are separate and therefore unclear to one another, I thought it time that we should meet, perhaps on neutral ground in the printed word. But language is a virus, as musician Laurie Anderson once observed, and words reveal the biases and limitations unbeknownst even to the one who crafts them. And so these words may dance with djinns, and if they or I have offended, it was not our intention. We seek the Moroccan condition of *hanan*—love, tenderness, compassion, forgiveness. We also seek understanding for our foibles, cursed but most certainly not without humor. Our best moments materialize when we laugh together with our djinns.

I think I have always lived with djinns. Each time I travel, my soul finds peace, and each time I return home all the more restless. It is not easy for my friends and family. I am always grateful for all that I have, but the inevitable quest, no matter how insignificant, seems to be my path and the path of my djinns.

King Solomon's testament records the peace that he made with djinns to build his temple. These genies are said to have borne the weight of the colossal blocks and columns that formed his architectural monument. Solomon then sent emissaries to the king of Arabia, by Arab request, to tame that country's deadly winds by capturing the perpetrating djinns in a vessel. The Queen of Sheba, it is written, was born of human and djinn lovemaking. While they may be destructive, blameworthy djinns also reflect an underlying creativity. At least my djinns and I are content to think so. These djinn-inspired fables hold a mirror to a creative wisdom common to the great desert religions: that people—kings, queens, neighbors, mosques, churches, temples—are capable of caring for others, trying to relieve rather than perpetuate suffering.

Morocco's potential for acceptance of beings of all natures, dispositions, colors, creeds, and ethnicities is worth noting over and over again. Perhaps there is a reason that the Moroccan kingdom was the first to recognize the United States after we gained our independence in the late eighteenth century. Perhaps there is a reason why we should encourage the Kingdom of Morocco's own young nation, which achieved its full independence in 1956. Laden with bureaucracy, illiteracy, poverty, and unemployment, Morocco's ancient soul and rich traditions persist.

I wrote these stories because I had to. Morocco's djinns exist in and around me, as I suspect they do for everyone, and we seek a balance as we continue to interact, whether we are here or there.

PART 2

Fes

We reached the ancient city as twilight melded into night. There were no stars, and no more than the thinnest splinter of a moon. A blanket of darkness shrouded the buildings, muffling the last words of the evening call to the faithful. Arriving at Fes by night is almost impossible to accurately describe. There's a sense that you're intruding upon something so secretive and so grave that you will be changed by the experience.

—Tahir Shah, *In Arabian Nights: A Caravan of Moroccan Dreams*

SPAIN
STRAIT OF GIBRALTAR
MEDITERRANEAN
SEA
FES
MOROCCO
FIGUIG

PROLOGUE

Taa lomo al achyae khayroun min jahliha.
(It is better to know a thing than not to know it.)

—Arab proverb

Poet David Whyte has observed that by writing, you discover what you didn't know that you knew. I might add that you also discover what you don't know.

These vignettes capture only glimmers of Moroccan life, registered by an innocent and ignorant eye. I realize that this collection is neither poetry nor travel essay, memoir, or blog. All four genres abound—bookstores are stocked; the Internet is replete. And yet the call to observe, record, reflect—to write—is so compelling that it must be answered.

It is human to inquire and to characterize, however faulty the perceptions. And once in a while, if we are lucky, we notice fissures in the constructs we create for ourselves to define our identities and others' and to shape our convictions. Through those tiny fractures, we glimpse new light. Cracks in our perceived foundations jostle us into new states of mindfulness.

Writing and reading are acts of faith, a willing exploration of the unknown, a search for a connection, a sharing of sensibilities. The contemplations allow us to chisel away at our preconceptions, to investigate the fissures. In doing so, we meet the human and beautiful in all its flaws.

Eight days in Fes affirmed what I did not know that I knew: that certitude of imperfection is innate to Moroccan culture. Our imperfect human condition is acknowledged in the concept of Allah, the perfect one. The call to prayer is a daily reminder. Mistakes weave their way into carpets and slip into ceramics as creative expressions that accept imperfection as our reality.

The arts embody these imperfections, our unfinished states. Through art, we struggle to complete ourselves, to comprehend, to find meaning. In the end, there may be none but what we ascribe. *Inshallah*, as God wills.

During my first trip to Morocco, I saw the country through the lens of five-star hotels, orchestrated, privileged, and protected. I made my second journey to Fes because I wanted to lift that romantic veil, to experience the imperfections. Life in the neighborhoods revealed both what I knew and did not know about Morocco and myself. To my surprise, I loved what I found beneath the veil and returned home all the more intoxicated.

These vignettes are once again offered in gratitude to my family and friends for their patience with my infatuations and restlessness. They are proffered with the deepest respect and love for my new Moroccan family. I hope that my misperceptions will be corrected in time; that my good intentions will shine through, however dimly; and that, *inshallah*, I shall return to my Moroccan friends one day to resume my lessons. So with boundless appreciation, I dedicate these writings to Zohar, Mohammed, Imad, Jaouad, Jacques, Fatima, Imane, Isham, Adil (known by many as Haj), Zineb, Bousta, Mohammed, Azziza, Hashem, Bouchra, Zohara, Yousef, Abas, Mustapha, Hafid, Abdul, Ahmed, and Abdellatif. Should they visit me one day, again I pray that my country will be as kind, revealing, and meaningful to them as Morocco has been to me.

THE CAR PARK

It is considered indelicate to take notice of what goes on next door. It's considered bad manners. In fact, one oughtn't to show oneself on the roof at all, and a man certainly not. Sometimes the womenfolk go up on the roofs, and they want to feel undisturbed.

—Elias Canetti, *The Voices of Marrakesh*

I am sitting in a *grande taxi* in the Ain Ahzletan parking lot. Because we think that we have arrived at our destination, we have flung the doors open, inadvertently allowing a throng of parking lot attendants to swarm into our space along with the late-afternoon heat that defeats the car's air-conditioning. Glaring sunshine bakes the rubbled car park yellow, silhouetting our uninvited guests as they loom into the taxi's interior. The lot marks the point where cars must stop, and the crush of people begins—life in the medina beyond it can be entered solely through a single archway by foot or donkey.

A host of young men with luggage carts buzz around the taxi, as the driver and I settle our account. We are receiving unwanted advice from a kind man who had escorted us from the new city to the old on his motorcycle after we had asked him for directions at a red light. We are also the center of annoying attention from a persistent, unofficial guide who vies with the slew of porters for my favor. The battery in my cell phone is running low, and I cannot seem to compose myself above the stifling din to dial the correct sequence of numbers to reach my purported destination. I'm sweating. Too much chaos has been generated by my greeting party, telling me how to dial, what paths to take to my hotel, how much to tip for services, where I should go on guided tours of the city, and above all, whom to avoid in the streets. The taxi driver is now a bit sullen, having lost complete control of our trip from Casablanca once he entered this city previously unknown to him. He had thought that a three-hour fare from his hometown here would be worth his while. It was—except during the last half hour of the journey when I

49

hadn't liked the French pornographic videos on his cell phone that he had tried to show me with delight before we hit city traffic. Our cheerful banter in broken French and Moroccan Arabic about olive trees and oleander, wheat fields and families, had taken a turn when he got bored with pictures of nieces and nephews and changed the channel to hot chicks.

My as-yet-unseen hotel is actually a *dar*, a home with an inner courtyard—the term *riad* is generally reserved for a house with an interior garden—and both types are currently undergoing renovations in the old city as private residences and bed-and-breakfasts. At this moment, I'm not sure that my *dar* actually exists. Someone was supposed to be there, awaiting my call to escort me to its door. Now, failing to reach the *dar* by taxi or by phone, I have no choice but to pay the disconsolate driver and tip the gracious motorcycle man with many thanks, decline the beseeching guide with the promise that I shall consider a tour the next day "for the sake of his five children," and hand my bags and myself over to a luggage porter who says that he knows the way.

My little adventure has just begun. *Good lord, what am I doing?*—the thought was fleeting and feeble in the face of needing to keep up with my rapidly vanishing bags on the cart ahead of me, in the search for some kind of roof to put over my head before sundown.

According to the directions, the *T* at the end of the first street through the medina archway appears quickly, at which point one takes a sharp left and follows the stone path to house number 76. That sharp left, however, leads to an endless decline downhill, deep into the medina, round many bends, followed by a turn left, then a right, then another left, then a right. "Let the road lead you down"—that's how the Irish typically give directions. The road usually turns out to be long, full of twists and turns, and utterly confounding because of multiple crossroad signs on a single post. Why should I have thought it would be different here? The main footpath curves past a million merchants staring at my ankles and more than happy to see a new customer in town. Eventually, it reaches a shaded, quiet corner of the medina—God knows where on my tiny, useless map. Pairs of men are spinning and stretching thin lines of silk thread along exterior walls of several houses for tailors' shops along the way. There is not a street sign in sight. Conflicting crossroad signs would have been welcome even as they forced me to painfully transliterate them from Arabic to English.

The footpath has progressively narrowed as it leads us to the *dar*, tucked among plaster-covered brick-and-mortar homes standing cheek by jowl three and four stories high. Small windows placed high in the walls and covered by curvilinear ironwork allow air to pass between exterior and interior but prevent nosy outsiders from looking in. I knock on the heavy wooden door and ring the bell. No one answers. No one. The porter is anxious to receive his tip and return to the other newly arrived innocents at the car park before sunset. He hates the

7/31/19

Lissa —

    Here's your* copy of
my dear old friend Anne's
book on her "pilgrimage"
to Morocco a few years
back. She has always been
a sensitive and observant
writer, and I hope
you'll enjoy getting
to know her a
bit.   Love, Goody

* I found a
copy online
quite easily. gct

WFAE42011 Tiger © isselee/Dreamstime.com

WWF

fact that I have no small money and only American dollar bills. I hate the fact that I am stranded with baggage in an unknown city in front of a locked door. A crowd of teenage boys starts to gather, each curious to speak to me in French or English, each claiming to know the absent proprietor. After much discussion and my pleading with the keeper of my bags not to depart until I find an open door, they offer to send scouts to find the owner at his office for me. The porter agrees to lead the expedition, shooting me a disdainful look and leaving me with his luggage cart.

There I am, abandoned on a gray stone path, surrounded by barren-looking buildings and gawking teenage boys. I have to move the cart continuously because its huge wheels and box block the paths of donkeys bearing bags of sand and lime for one final clomp up and down the streets at the end of their belabored day.

I decide to calm down. The boys and I start to laugh at my American dollars—"Good for taping to the wall, madame, for display" (exchange banks are a bit of a stretch for them at this point in their lives). We talk about the annual sacred music festival that has just begun its sixteenth year in this ancient city. The boys love music; some sing in their school choirs. One, a shy smaller boy with crossed blue eyes and a dour expression, has been ominously lurking in a corner, watching the spectacle of my arrival. He turns out to be famous among his peers for his songs. As our mood relaxes, we begin to encourage him. Suddenly, he smiles and lifts his head to the Lord. The beautiful purity of his voice carries an Arabic aria to the heavens above a backbeat of braying donkeys and their shouting drivers, howling babies, and crowing roosters. We stand transported by its utter loftiness. I am moved to tears by its tenderness, matched only by the sweet nature of his teenage buddies, slowly revealing itself as time passes.

The proprietor, looking all of about seventeen, arrives. He is tall and muscular, with dark bedroom eyes and a mouth full of silver braces. I borrow twenty *dirhams* from him to pay the disgruntled porter; I give the tender teenagers dollar bills to paste to their walls. My proprietor unlocks the forbidding door. Leaving the boys with a profuse exchange of thanks and laughter, I walk across the threshold into my home for the next week.

Imad, the young proprietor, asks if I am okay. I start to cry, tell him "I'm fine, just tired. Thank you," and smoke a cigarette. "Poor madame." He pats me on the shoulder. We laugh as I pronounce that I am indeed crazy for being here where no one who knows me knows where I am. I clear my tears; we smile and shrug. Then we zigzag up a set of steep, uneven stairs to my room, deliver my cumbersome bags, and then follow another bewildering set of left-and-right turns to stagger up another set of high and narrow steps to the rooftop.

And there the city lies below—sunbaked, dusty, and teeming with construction workers, contractors, merchants, shoppers, weavers, butchers, farmers, families, cell phones, and cats. In the approaching evening light, a minaret rises before me within a stone's throw, and beyond it, sheep bleat on a hillside leading to a fourteenth-century fortress and tombs of the Merinid dynasty. Rooftop terraces of countless homes with satellite dishes stretch between the hills and me. Stray kittens taunt each other as they trespass across the *riad* roofs set closely together like pieces of a puzzle, terraces and walls linking one house to the next. On the roof just below me to the right, an unveiled mother plays with her baby, shaded by a sheet draped across the corner of her terrace. To my left, the higher roof of the adjacent house affords a view of me, a stranger in the neighborhood. A diaper, discarded from a tiny window on the top floor, has caught on the ironwork and hangs precariously over the heads of those who pass by on the street below. Life in that house was never silent during my entire stay—shouts of children playing, a baby giggling by day and wailing at bedtime, people bantering, and cell phones constantly ringing in competition with a rooster that never slept but crowed twenty-four hours a day.

I am overlooking a world-heritage site, Morocco's center of Islam, an ancient city of astonishing artisanship, a warren of houses and shops certain to confuse the cleverest navigator, a site protected by UNESCO, the baking noonday sun, and shining stars each night. The panicky first minutes of my arrival are starting to transmute, unfolding into centuries of revelations.

I am standing alone on that rooftop terrace, listening to the calls to prayer as they resound in a chorus from all corners of the city, broadcast from minarets that lace the lives of the Fassi below, ensconced within their age-old city walls under an incomprehensibly vast sky. Thus begins my personal pilgrimage. I am in Fes.

THE SOUK

He was thin and wiry, squint-eyed behind his glasses as he pleaded with me. He'd scrunch up his face and rub his short, cropped hair every time he approached me. "Please, madame, just step inside a moment to look. Just to look." His shop was stuffed full of more objects than the eye could possibly register—bracelets, teapots, ceramics, rugs. In fact, he worked twin souks, shops facing each other across the main path to and from the *dar* that I temporarily called home. "If you like this one here, you may like that one over there even better." Day after day, he would try to entice me. Day after day, I swore that I was in a hurry and would stop tomorrow. "J'ai pressée, domaine peut-être."

Though his souks were hard to distinguish from all the others that lined the street—shops with barkers simply trying to make a sale—there was something about his particular determination and slightly crooked demeanor that attracted me. I finally accepted his invitation, one that led to completely unforeseen wonders of camel-bone jewelry, wheel-turned pitchers and plates, colorful shawls, and hammered brass pots for mint tea. Even more engaging was the conversation. His name was Mustapha; the actual owner's name was Mohammed. We were introduced during subsequent exchanges as the days went by. Of course, Mustapha loved Washington, DC, and our President Obama. Of course, I bought a few things from him—a silver cuff for my cousin and a bracelet made of bits from an old camel's skeleton for me. As we conversed, he would watch my eyes scan his shop and alight on something of interest. He never gave up hope that I would relent and purchase that little teapot, presented again and again during that week, until his boss finally put an end to the pestering. Once he let the obsession go, he shifted his focus to insisting on making a present for me. I chose a small two-piece, hand-painted bowl that dropped cigarette butts into its base while holding ashes on top, at a much-reduced price. It was blue and white, the traditional colors of Fes ceramics, made from the region's gray clay.

Mustapha's days were long. Shops open early in the morning and only begin to close between ten and midnight. No matter what time I strolled by, he was there. At first, I tried to dodge him, sneaking by when he was preoccupied with a potential sale. By the end of the week, I was seeking him out to exchange pleasantries.

We found common ground in fractured French, though he was patient with my baby Arabic. We agreed about how privileged it must be to travel far from home. Most of all, we talked about how short life was and how beautiful art is and how important it is to be happy. I wasn't looking for anything in particular in his shops as I gazed over his wares, but his word, *happy*, resonated deeply. "Ferhana?" he would ask each day as I walked by. "Oui, 'ferhana,'" I would reply. "Et vous, monsieur, 'ferhan?'" Yes, we were both delightfully happy with our little greeting several times a day as I traversed the main route of the medina. We were happy in those precise moments. We piqued the curiosity of other tourists within earshot, thereby indirectly encouraging them to step inside his souks. And I was sad the last day to say good-bye. He wished me a bon voyage and much happiness in life. I wished the same for him and many sales, including brass pots for mint tea, and many more conversations with those who passed by. We said farewell my last morning and meant it. Later that afternoon, when I made my final trek up the "big slope" (*Talaa Kebira*) from *dar* to car park, lugging my bags stuffed with jewelry, ceramics, and *djellabas*—my own little souk—he was nowhere to be seen.

SACRED MUSIC

The annual sacred music festival in Fes enjoyed its eighteenth year in 2012. It was inspired after the first Gulf War by a cleric seeking to season the cosmic soup with a pinch of peace and harmony. Each year thereafter, astonishing musicians from all corners of the world arrive to perform for audiences, who clap and sway to the sounds of Pan-African, Asian, European, and Islamic rhythms.

Concerts take place in Bab al Makina within the ramparts of Bab Makhzen, leading to the royal palace and arsenal built in 1886. Breezes blow through the open courtyard, and swallows lilt overhead in the evening air. Dusk settles and then night falls, bringing with it a veil of stars. A trio of electric Malian guitars release ancestral blues disseminating from Niger River basins to the Mississippi Delta and floating to the heavens. From Zanzibar, an immaculate troupe of Sufi singers—striking in their crisp white robes, red vests, and fezzes—perform choreographed chants of transporting elegance. Their gracefully synchronized praises of Allah contain the seeds of American gospel music and slave songs. When the Sufi voices fall silent, tall, muscular athletes take the stage, beating large Burundian kettledrums with changing rhythms, punctuated by gravity-defying leaps and dance.

French, German, Russian, Spanish, and Arabic languages interlace the audience. Visiting dignitaries in dark suits share mint tea within the vendors' tents. The hip wear jeans and drink Cokes. Little black dresses and strappy gold sandals are outdone by young girls who cover their heads and bodies in black-and-white prints of the finest fabrics, accented by dramatic kohl-lined eyes and stiletto heels. Large video screens broadcast close-ups of the entertainers. At intermission, they feature images of the Moroccan flag—a distinctive single green star against a red background—flying before a backdrop of the county's dramatic landscapes: snow-frosted mountains, valleys of date palms, salty ocean waves, and cinnamon deserts.

For those who cannot afford tickets, public squares offer free concerts, which can be heard in the distance. Proceeds from the music festival, supplemented by the government, make it possible for all citizens and visitors to enjoy these late-night revelries. For several evenings in June, the Fassi celebrate song, as international music resounds from all quarters of the city beneath unifying stars.

My ticketed concert has ended, and I step out of the tranquil courtyard to meet Haj who is escorting me home. We had met during my previous trip to Fes when he helped guide our group through the old city. He is the lord of the medina who knows everyone, and he has kindly offered to meet me two nights in a row after finishing his tours ("from Chicago! Oklahoma! New York! And Spain!"). It will be a long walk to my *dar*, because his friends and colleagues stop to greet him at every step. Last night he introduced me to his friend the butcher, who at 11:00 p.m. was just closing up shop. Tonight we are accompanied by two of my new acquaintances. They checked into the *dar* today, and because they are still adjusting to their first day in Fes, they appreciate being guided from the concert hall to our neighborhood in a dark corner of the city. She is American; he is Danish. They met on a train in Mexico. I introduce them to Haj, who leads us back toward the medina.

As we enter Bab Boujeloud Square, a spacious plaza northeast of the concert hall, a group of Sufi musicians entrances the people gathered there. The entire square is in motion. The air, filled with bobbing metallic helium balloons, smells like popped corn. People are swaying and spinning. Toddlers grab each other's arms and try to dance.

The crowd swallows us up in seconds. Haj grabs my hand, I grab the American's, and she grabs her Danish boyfriend's as we wend our way. Dodging and weaving slowly from one side of the plaza to the other, we pass a row of beaming children in wheelchairs. We share their joy, exchanging greetings as we inch past them. Boys about Haj's height stare at him; their parents first look down to him and then up in surprise at me, his girlfriend for the evening. Then their eyes fall on the young American behind me, dancing as she maneuvers through the throngs, and rise yet again as they look up into the face of her towering boyfriend. We are quite the foursome, stars of our own Fellini movie. The city's shortest and tallest men serve as our asymmetrical bookends, while my modest shirt that covers my middle-aged body cannot compete with the American girl's cleavage, bouncing merrily in her cotton baby-doll dress. Indeed, we are a sight, doing our share to contribute to the carnival atmosphere. When we reach the Bab Boujeloud, the Blue Gate, we decide to stop for a drink. Haj takes us to his favorite café. He orders mint tea; our friends buy some sponge bread soaked in honey from a stall across the way. The café is filled with men; a few female tourists have chosen to sit in the adjacent one. The lights are bright, the food sweet and sticky, and the crowd boisterous. Drumbeats echo from the town squares throughout the city. A night in Fes—inspired, unpredictable, incongruous. *Ferhana*. I am happy.

LUNCH

"Whoever you are," she said, "Morocco takes you in. Before you know it, you have a home and friends, and you've forgotten your troubles."
—Tahir Shah, *The Caliph's House*

In Morocco, I am usually on time or early. Quite ironic, given that I am habitually late for everything in my own country. My husband is fond of saying that I shall die ten minutes after the official pronouncement. I try, I really do, to mind the clock, because to be late is to be rude, but to no avail. So one would assume that Moroccan time would suit me perfectly. It is lunar, and all things happen as they will, when they will—a concept far more in sync with my own natural rhythms. Nevertheless, being completely unencumbered for eight days in Fes, I find that I have time to be punctual. Haj has invited me to his home for lunch with his family. I am honored. When he says that he will meet me outside my door at one o'clock, I am ready.

He is late. I feel conspicuous while loitering in front of my own house, and so I step back inside to the courtyard instead. I am wondering if lunch is one of those polite Moroccan promises that never come to pass. Eventually there is a knock on the door. I am not where I am supposed to be, so now I am the one who is late, naturally.

I open the door to be greeted by a man who looks so much like Haj that I stare a second too long, scanning him to process the information. The same coloring, eyes, nose, mouth, and teeth. The same stature. I smile as I stare. Then I look into the exotic eyes of a taller woman standing next to him. She grins at me, a bit uncertain; I grin back, completely confused.

Though we have little language in common, it becomes clear that Haj is running late and has sent his brother, Hashem, and sister, Zineb, in his place. As we blithely set off together—my new friends and their newfound captive—they stop immediately at a pay phone stall to call Haj to translate, to be sure I understand. Soon we are climbing the slope of Talaa Kebira, the main street. Zineb slips her arm through mine and tells me I am beautiful in a mix of Arabic English. I return the compliment, stunned by her loveliness and warmth. Hashem just looks at me and laughs infectiously, as he continues to do throughout the afternoon.

I could have taken a taxi or met them somewhere in the medina. But lunch means that Haj is the host and I am the guest right from the start, whatever the time. His siblings seem genuinely amused by their assignment to fetch me despite what must be a terrible inconvenience and interruption in their day. We hail a taxi and head to their neighborhood in a comparatively poor section surrounding the grand hotels and gardens on the hills overlooking the city.

Women on their block certainly notice that I am an interloper. Children are thrilled. Men ignore me. Small doors and windows interrupt an endless facade of sand-colored stucco walls that link one small house to the next along the street. Zineb suddenly stops in front of one door and unlocks it.

The doors of wealthier Moroccan homes typically open to a small right-angled foyer that blocks a view into the ornate house itself. Haj's door opens directly to a main room that leads to the kitchen on one side and bedrooms on the other. A soap opera is playing on the portable TV. The walls are white, trimmed in blue. Opposite is a room, a salon, lined with cobalt-blue and gold divans, and a large octagonal table on wheels, draped with a deep-blue-and-gold embroidered tablecloth. A red oriental carpet—an Arabian floral and paisley pattern—covers the floor down the length of the room. Sheer blue curtains flutter in the breeze. There are no images on the walls except for a framed illuminated page from the Koran.

One by one, siblings appear from all angles to greet me. Mohammed, the eldest son, is waiting in the salon. His heart condition has made him very ill and unable to work for the past two years. Two other sisters join him. Zineb introduces them as Bouchra and Zohara. They beckon me to sit, and while we wait for Haj, I ask if I can help the eldest sister, Azziza, who has not yet appeared but is tending food in the kitchen. Zineb sits close by my side, thumbing through her English-Arabic textbook, intent on exchanging lessons with me. Hashem plants himself across from us, still laughing and tickled by the scene.

It is now two o'clock, and Haj has still not arrived. Then the outside door opens, but instead of Haj, it frames a tall man in a dark *djellaba*—a Moroccan robe with pointed hood. He wears a skullcap and carries a long walking stick. His shadowy figure fills the doorway. Haj's father. He is imposing; I am nervous. He disappears without introduction—I am afraid that *I* am the imposition, which he simply cannot bear. But when he emerges again after some time, he has changed into his best household *djellaba* at his daughters' insistence. He has a wizened face, a slight gray beard, and eyes that look as though they have seen too much. They light up, however, as he smiles when I try my best to say in Moroccan Arabic "Peace be with you, nice to meet you"—a genuine stretch from my disarming trick of singing my ABCs to a children's tune ("Alif, baa, taa, thaa, jiim, haa, khaa . . ."). He shakes my hand and welcomes me to Morocco and into his house. *He* thanks *me* over and over again for coming. We persuade Azziza to leave the kitchen, and I thank *her* for all the shopping and the cooking that she has done that morning. Our talk is limited, but I can tell by the glint in her eye that she knows I appreciate the extra work that a luncheon guest means for the eldest daughter and keeper of the hearth.

Eight children in all, four boys and four girls, now grown men and women, live together with Bousta, their father, in this home. Haj and Hashem work; Zineb, Bouchra, and Zohara study at the university. Yousef, the youngest son, will miss lunch because of his job as a car mechanic, though business is slow. Azziza runs the house. They all tend to Mohammed, so thin and frail and unwell, though imbued with good humor. He sports a baseball cap that says "Italia." Everyone wears jeans and T-shirts, except Azziza in black velour stretch capris and Bousta in his beautiful brown *djellaba*. His children range in age from twenty-one to thirty-two. Bousta, they joke, is eighty if not one hundred (he is actually sixty-four). Their mother is deceased, I learn, when Zineb gestures to indicate that she is now part of the universe and not on the planet any longer.

Affectionate teasing rules the day, especially with their father. When Haj finally walks through the door, there are hugs and kisses and giggling, even when he sternly makes us all take off our shoes, as we are meant to do in the salon. Zineb points to her sneakers, my shoes, and the carpet, laughing at her naughty conspiracy that did not go unnoticed by her brother. I compliment the carpet and am told apologetically that it is machine-made, for handmade would have been too expensive. I sheepishly remove my shoes. Haj places them by the door.

His family has set the table with deep-blue napkins the color of the curtains, the banquette tassels, and the floral pattern of the tablecloth. They cover it with transparent plastic to catch crumbs and spills. They serve a choice of still or sparkling water, purchased just because Haj knows that I like it. Hashem disappears just prior to lunch but returns with a new travel pack of Tempo tissues, a present for me to begin the meal.

Azziza brings in a large serving dish displaying an array of Moroccan "salads" fit for a sultan: cold beets, carrots, tomatoes and cucumbers, eggplant, green beans with preserved lemon, grilled chicken kabobs, sliced hard-boiled eggs, and bread. I keep thanking them, the father keeps thanking me, Haj keeps insisting that I am forever welcome in their home, Hashem keeps laughing, Zineb continues to show me phrases from her book, and Bouchra and Zohara quietly smile at me. Mohammed eats little of a special meal prepared for him but brightens at the mention of soccer and the New York Yankees. Azziza is pleased that I recognize her efforts on my behalf. We gesture wildly when our spotty Arabic, English, French, and Spanish fail us. We use the numerical keypads of our cell phones to indicate our ages, in between taking pictures of one another.

We finish the meal, and dishes are cleared, followed by a commotion in the kitchen. I look at the clock, remembering that I have a concert to attend at

4:00 p.m. Plenty of time. A fine lunch, indeed. Haj had asked me last night if I preferred vegetables, chicken, or beef if I should visit his home. I said vegetables would be lovely and requested that he call his sister to forewarn her. He declared that we would have beef—the most expensive choice—reaching her immediately on the phone. Today when the chicken and vegetables were served, I was relieved.

But wait. Azziza is not cleaning up the kitchen after all. When she rejoins the family, she carries a huge platter of couscous smothered in a deliciously gooey concoction of golden raisins, honey, lemon, and cinnamon. "Kul, kul, kul," everyone chants at me. Eat, eat, eat. We share the platter, each taking forkfuls of couscous, directly from dish to mouth. I take small bites, but the siblings shovel larger ones toward me. Further conversation reveals that Mohammed had worked in the international transport business. Bouchra is a medaled long-distance runner. Zohara studies English literature. Kul, kul, kul! We eat the afternoon away.

And then another surprise. As we finally make our way toward the center of the platter, we reach a tender pot roast hidden within the golden mountain. Beef for a special occasion! Kul, kul, kul! Couscous is a round semolina grain that serves many people very well. It is often underestimated because of its ubiquitous nature, though it daily proves its ability to harbor succulent surprises of untold riches. We do our best to devour the meat but leave just enough so that the cook does not have to prepare dinner tonight or lunch tomorrow. Azziza and I steal an appreciative glance at one another. She disappears again. Haj and Hashem, full and happy, recline on the banquettes. Haj asks me if I want to smoke, remembering that I sneaked a cigarette in the café with my tour-guide friends last night. No need today.

A plate of fresh fruit provides the finishing touch. The honeydew melon is so sweet, surrounded by bananas, grapes, and apples. Refreshing. My hosts insist that I share part of a banana, and though I say "M'kein m'shkil" (No problem), finding room for one more bite is a challenge.

It is now time for the crowning ceremony. Zineb lights some incense. Bousta has offered to make mint tea for us, using his wife's brass tea service, a wedding gift. It is well past four o'clock, and my concert has commenced. While it would be a pleasure, listening to North-African and French music cannot compare to the honor granted to me here today. I easily let it go, distracted by brass pots brimming with great squares of sugar, mounds of fresh mint, loose tea leaves, and hot water all circumscribed by a big brass tray. Bousta masterfully prepares the libation, capping the performance by pouring a long stream of steaming tea into tiny etched glasses from great heights. We toast to everyone's health. He stands, bows, and puts his hand over his heart to welcome me once again. He shies away from my wanting to give him a kiss on the cheek. But he looks me in the eye as he kisses my hand with great formality and sincere friendliness. I am charmed.

Then he vanishes into the bedroom for an afternoon nap. Hashem, Bouchra, and Zohara are off to claim what remains of the late afternoon. It is after five o'clock. Mohammed needs to rest. Haj needs to make some phone calls for his tours tonight. Zineb, Azziza, and I decide to go for a walk to see the view of Fes from the gardens above the city. Zineb and I put on our shoes and wait for Azziza to dress in her *hijab* and *djellaba*—both made of fabrics woven with swirling pink, orange, and purple patterns. Covered by a head scarf and robe, her beautiful dark curls, textured yellow T-shirt, and black pants will remain a complete secret to outsiders. But as Haj has promised and the afternoon has revealed, I am now an insider, one of the family. The sisters—one modern, one traditional—hold my hands as we walk along the wide boulevard leading to the Merinid tombs.

Before I finally leave them for good in a flurry of hugs and kisses, they give me a silver bracelet with beads of green glass, the color of Islam, and a charm in the form of the hand of Fatima, the protective emblem of the Prophet's daughter. It is nearly six o'clock before Haj and I catch a taxi back to the medina. We have escaped time today, or rather, we have plumbed its essence. As moments have unfolded, one blending into the other and streaming us along, time has revealed its meaning. It is a great gift of love.

Cultural Ablutions

"Morocco is the place where all religions live freely," he said. "There were Jews here two-thousand years ago, long before the Arabs. Many have gone to Israel now, but in their hearts they are Moroccan."

—Tahir Shah, *In Arabian Nights:*
A Caravan of Moroccan Dreams

A tiny synagogue tucked among irregular blocks of pale clay-colored houses is a quiet testimony to a singular history of Judaism in Fes. Today, Bet Ha-Kenesset Rabbi Shlomo Ibn Danan, or the Aben Danan Synagogue as it is known by the Arab community, is a reminder of the cycles of persecution and protection withstood by its congregations through the centuries.

Built in the seventeenth century, the synagogue stands in the historic center of the city, beside homes and shops of merchants and tradespeople and approached through Fes's narrow corridors—often one person wide. The synagogue witnessed attacks on the Jewish community and property during the eighteenth century, followed by a renovation during the 1870s and a restoration in 1999. Inside the entrance, plaques now bear the names of Muslim and Jewish cultural ministers and donors who supported its preservation.

A guide will show the plaques to you, emphasizing his fragile country's wish for tolerance among all cultural and religious traditions. He insists, he persuades, and he nearly convinces his audience, as if to will tolerance into reality. His example—this modest building—yearns to be a place of pride, though in need of more care than seems possible at the moment.

Jewish and Arab people lived together in the Moroccan region long before Fes was founded 800 CE. Oppression during the tenth and eleventh centuries was followed by periods of peaceful coexistence under the Berber dynasty through the 1400s, when the Jewish quarter was solidly established in the city.

The quarter is called the *mellah*, which derives from *al-Mallah*, Arabic for *salt*. Various legends explain the term. One story relates to the salt trade, which was largely overseen in this quarter. Another tale tells of an angry local pasha who salted the heads of his enemies, impaled on sticks to serve as warnings to his challengers.

Now largely populated by Arabs, the *mellah* once offered sanctuary for Hebrew people—comfort for a group unlike Morocco's majority. But the mere existence of the *mellah* might symbolize the dark side of human nature. Like people choose to live together, but societies also segregate those who are perceived as different. Our deepest instincts may well be fearful and tribal. For centuries, the *mellah* housed Jewish populations, whose numbers dwindled dramatically with emigrations to Israel after 1948 and again in 1967.

From the street, a tiny doorway leads into the synagogue. Light from high windows and chandeliers illuminates a central room. Blue and white tiles surround the walls, dark wooden beams support the ceiling, and intricate ceramic patterns stretch across the floor. Simple benches fill the center of the room, all within view of the Torah housed in a wooden cupboard. Above, a balcony for women projects over the right side of the room. Below, down a winding stairwell, a bathing room stands ready for bridal purifications before weddings.

The command to build a *mikvah* as the foundation for a synagogue speaks of an ancient orthodox Jewish tradition. Water for sacred cleansing. Mosques contain ablution pools. Christians practice baptism in the name of St. John. The *mikvah*—a natural collection of water—provides an immersion site for the ritual purification of men, women, and converts of the Jewish faith. Here, women in the congregation bathed the bride-to-be. The ritual bath is expected of Muslim brides too, having evolved in Morocco into many prenuptial visits to the *hammam*, as well as a milk bath in preparation for the wedding ceremonies that last four to seven days.

In the darkness of the abandoned synagogue's underground *mikvah*, mosquitoes now float through the humid air. Still, the scene invites images of nuptial preparations and wedding celebrations. Delacroix's North African sketch of a Jewish bride costumed for her wedding crosses the imagination. She sits cross-legged on a cushion, slippers discarded on the carpet before her. A flowing gown with billowing sleeves is brushed with orange, red, and blue washes. Jewels frame her face. She is pensive, burdened beneath the beautiful tiered headdress and blue mantle that inscribe her body against a blank background.

How many sacred immersions—ablutions—have been performed here over the centuries, now haunted by phantom images of women purifying the bride beneath the synagogue and men later accepting her into their family during the marriage ritual on its main floor? How many families have meted out the passages of their lives centered in this building, grounded in this neighborhood?

No longer the site of active worship or sacred rites, the synagogue remains a historic marker, a public monument. Judaic wooden platforms and screens now share space with Islamic wrought-iron archways and window grids.

Always on the official guide's tour and bathed in light for visitors, the synagogue attests to history's lessons and our continual ablutions for penance and enlightenment.

CORK TREES, STORKS, AND TRUFFLES

To make friends with *djinns*, you offer them milk or powdered henna, or burn incense.

—Suzanna Clarke, *A House in Fez*

Cork trees provide an enchanted oasis along the *autoroute* that transports the traveler between Fes in the northeast and the bustling cities of Rabat and Casablanca along the northwest coast of Morocco. Arid hills enriched by silver olive groves and golden wheat fields flatten after Meknes as you approach Rabat. Eventually, a coastline of sand and blue sea emerges on your right side and green woodland on your left. As you drive along the road that they share, the conjoined treescape and seascape interrupt your concentration by their bewitching paradox. The sea air is humid—mist obscures the view of waves and beach—while sunlight clarifies the dry cork forest, warming the cool darkness.

There is magic here. It casts a spell over you before you are even aware of what you are seeing. The feeling is electric, magnetic, seducing you out of your daily preoccupations into a mystical ancient place. Once you awaken to this enchanted state of childlike wonder, you discover the supernatural.

The cork trees rise before you, their dark leaves and narrow branches hanging thick and heavy over gnarled trunks. They stand like primeval ancestors of lighter-hearted willows transformed by some angry god into their opposite: alluring, wild, dark, and a bit foreboding. Legend says that the cork oak lives five hundred years; its bark can be harvested without harm to the tree every decade or so. The evergreen sirens that call to you today, however, guard their contents and grow unassaulted, creating forests of shade and respite for the occasional donkey, dog, or truffle-seeker.

In February, you can spot the harvesters, collecting and covering small mounds of truffles to dot the forest bed. The truffle-gatherers are as thin and ghostlike as the rangy trees, barely leaving a footprint or trace of their presence as they root out their delectables. Food for the soul indeed.

In June, a few truffle mounds remain, but there is no hint that human beings ever walked this place. It is fodder for fairy tales; djinns certainly live here, tucked among the truffles and hiding within the cork trunks, keeping time to the temporal but answering to the eternal.

Other cultures might call them tricksters or leprechauns; some call them devils, but Moroccan djinns are spirits, genies, said to inhabit a universe largely invisible but parallel to human life. They usually enter our human world to tease and taunt. Here, in the cork woods, they do not invite you to share their space as much as they draw you in irresistibly. You find yourself captive and, in spite of yourself, hypnotized by the ambience of their habitat: undeniably tangible, incredibly still, invisibly animated, and definitely haunted.

Indeed, the human world of trucks and vans and cars racing along the autoroute between cities must seem curious to djinns, and they lure us from it despite their reclusive natures. Perhaps it is the collision of human and djinn energies within the cork forest that generates the magic.

You are a guest in the land of cork trees and truffles, and as you marvel over its mysteries, a stork soars through the air at close range. You look down an endless beak to catch its eye—it is most certainly watching you. You follow the graceful, aerodynamic lines of this gangly elliptical bird as it stretches its long legs and glides on wide wings to a resting place. Then you spot another and another. Storks nest in pairs to raise their young. They perch along the road atop cell phone towers and tollbooths and tempt you to the cork forest that is their kingdom. They colonize the ancient ruins and tombs at Chellah nearby, building huge nests on top of abandoned minarets. They populate northern European folktales. They are symbols of abundance and good fortune. They deliver babies to human families. They gather centuries of fantasies and fables into focus for you, here in their homeland.

They embody, effortlessly, all that is illusion and reality here. You inhale the charmed air with them.

But then, as the autoroute carries you away, road signs appear marking the way to Rabat and Casablanca. You exhale, blink, and the cork trees, storks, and truffles vanish. The spell is broken. Still, despite your disenchantment, you have learned that this magical land will lie in wait for your return.

MOROCCAN MAGIC

Just what is so magical about Morocco? The gulf between rich and poor is wide and deep. The country's breadbasket surrounding Meknes is ripe with olive groves, grape orchards, and wheat fields. But the land is parched and dry during the long hot summer months, and the rainy season in the spring can be unpredictably torrential, stretching into June to drench the crops. Tiny adobe homes dot the landscape or cluster into small towns. Smoky industrial plants can be seen around the horizon. On Fridays, solitary men carrying their prayer rugs walk long distances down country roads to the nearest mosque. In the city, enrobed elderly women watch from within their black *chadors* as they follow a path to the old medina, passing an urban basketball court under construction.

Unemployment is high, and poverty is rampant, yet the king is reputed to be good. His outlook and marriage to a computer scientist have done much for women's rights. Still, it is said that visas are granted to the rich to promote tourism but denied the poor to prevent emigration. Eighteen-year-old kids are abandoning family businesses and ancient artisan traditions to risk their lives aboard boats to Spain by night, hoping for a better life but sometimes drowning in the process.

Education is compulsory. Children are multilingual by age six. They study French and classic Arabic from the start in school, eventually adding Spanish or English to their curriculum. Young women outnumber men in university enrollment, and street alleys are crowded with guys hanging out with nothing to do.

Oriental romanticism among tourists and expatriates is alive and well. The main square in Marrakech pulses day and night with exotic life: storytellers and beggars, monkeys, reptiles, and snake charmers who pose for photographs for a few *dirhams*. Caravans of camel-trekkers seek life under the Saharan stars in prepared Bedouin tents with full-service meals. British, French, Australians, and Americans are helping to rebuild the world-heritage medina in old Fes, renovating *dars* by day and gathering by night at an alcohol-free café owned by an expat couple seeking a new life.

Guns are forbidden, but robberies at knifepoint are not uncommon. Still, neighborhoods are very safe by US standards, and merchants, as well as children, know who belongs and who does not, even watching out for tourists staying in the local *riads*. A network of highly orchestrated official guides and underground police ensure the safety of their charges, graciously meeting every demand without a hint of underworld crime that might disturb a romantic experience scented by orange oil and rose petals.

You are told to watch your pockets but might forget on starlit nights in early June, when songs echo from public squares across Fes, competing with calls to prayer. Fassi pack the plazas, balloons fill the carnival air, and children dance between tourists holding hands so as not to lose each other as they navigate the crowds. Sufi musicians sing themselves into trances at these free concerts offered for those who cannot afford tickets to the halls for the annual sacred music festival. Entranced hippies, young and old, spin across the plaza to their own internal tunes from other cultures.

To a person, the Moroccans whom I met speak from their hearts. Whether age seven or seventy, they are quick to welcome you and express affection. A child on the street races up to me—a stranger—takes my hand, and asks for a kiss. She is six. Her mother smiles. I share a taxi with a grandfather and a preteenager, who graciously says "Benvenue a Maroq," inquires about what I have seen, asks my age, and sends his regards to my family. Little boys and girls scurry after me, and I chase them a bit along the footpaths while their parents simply laugh. Two grown sisters—one wearing a *hijab* and *djellaba*, the other in jeans—take my hands to walk with me and tell me *I* am beautiful. Men, while hollering aggressively at each other for bad driving on the highways, show genuine affection in the cafés where they sit side by side, whispering while watching the world pass by. Teenage boys from conservative families seem goofy and love-struck, grateful for attention once their beloved sisters suddenly step behind the veil. Liberal girls streak their hair and want to practice their English while staring at your curls and clothes and shoes. Families of all ages live together in small spaces, often relying on the livelihood of a single son and brother. The elderly are not abandoned but stay part of the households that they established.

Life spills forth in the crazed marketplaces teeming with spices, peaches, squawking chickens, and fresh trotters bound like firewood for sale. The heads of camels, calves, and goats mark the butchers' stalls. Women prepare flat bread and sponge cake on wheels in their tiny shops. Leavened bread is carried on palettes from houses to communal bakeries and back. Cottage industries exist behind the doors of private homes, where delicacies are prepared for local restaurants. Merchants offer mint tea and lively conversation in their souks, then lead you to special, secret shops, usually run by their siblings, whether they have made a sale or not. In higher-end carpet and antique stores, you negotiate on the floor with a salesman but finalize the contract with the director, often a woman, behind the desk.

Mosques and shrines offer sanctuary for both genders from the hot midday sun—cool, shaded spaces for meditation or reading. The head *imam* is a man who has studied the Koran for at least fourteen years, if not his entire lifetime; his is a government position. Muezzins call you to prayer at dawn, early and late afternoon, sundown, and before midnight. You may stop, face east, and pray; or you may just go about your business. You might choose to simply gather yourself in the moment. It is hard to be oblivious to the powerful voices echoing across the stone city, lifting you from the overwhelming din of daily life and reminding you of something larger than yourself and even more mysterious. *Inshallah*, as God wills.

The common wish from a Moroccan whom you have just met is that you enjoy a long and happy life. This kind blessing from virtual strangers is magical. *Ihamdu'illa* (praise be to God), that magic is manifested every day in the clash of ancient traditions and contemporary values, muezzins' prayers and Moroccan hip-hop, limbless beggars and fine leather jackets. On any given day—whether dry as dust or in a balmy mist—relentless suffering and good humor, chaos and compassion are knit together to nourish the miraculous heartbeat of this country.

EIGHT DAYS IN FES

Maybe it was because I always enjoyed slow motion, and dreamed of life
as a quiet and unhurried dance.

—Fatima Mernissi, *Dreams of Trespass:*
Tales of a Harem Girlhood

"But what did you *do* alone for eight days?" a colleague asked me upon my
return. "Did you get a tan?" asked another. Visions of serene moments spent on
a rooftop in the glaring sunshine or under the stars come to mind. Arabic and
English lessons exchanged with the boys who ran the *dar* are now memorable
vignettes. "Mezyan!" (Good!) "Mumtaz!" (Excellent!)

"Oh, Anne, I taught you that word yesterday. Why can't you remember it?"
Jaouad would instruct one day, and Imad the next, as I scanned the files in my
brain to conjugate verbs or name children, stars, or roosters in Arabic.

My friends in the States weren't the only ones who wondered what I was doing.

Imad thought I was too tense and needed to go to his gym, Lady Sport, and
see his favorite masseuse. Jaouad told me to stop smoking and wanted me to come
to his salon so he could style my hair. Ahmed, a man who crowds his life guiding
tourists in the medina by day but seeks sanctuary at his mountain retreat by
night, was concerned that I might be lonely. "Oh no, you are by yourself on your
rooftop," he would say sympathetically over the phone.

I saw blue mist burn off the valley as the sun rose each morning. I watched
light grow long and golden as the sun set each night. Goats grazed before me
on the hillside. Entrancing Sufi songs filled my senses in the evenings. I learned
about Mecca's cycles of neglect and rebirth over the course of two millennia
from an Arab professor's French lecture beneath a centuries-old live oak in a
museum courtyard.

I was witnessing a renaissance in a medieval city firsthand. I toured old Fes's restorations—*dars* being rehabilitated from rubble to *zellij*. I discovered where all the donkeys loaded with lime and sand had been going all week long.

Imad had shared Dar Othmane's scrapbook with me during breakfast one morning—photos of the two-year transformation of the house from ramshackle into a simple bed-and-breakfast. A fountain of handmade mosaics now graces its small courtyard, as colored glass panes filter daylight into the overlooking rooms. I keep a tiny eight-point star tucked in my purse, a mosaic tile given to me by my guide at the pottery factory, which he hopes one day will lead to my owning my own fountain in a Fes courtyard. I can begin building it one tile at a time, he said, promising that when I finally order the entire fountain for my *dar*, he will throw in a few small ceramic pots for free.

After studying Imad's images of the *dar's* metamorphosis, I met Hafid for a tour of other homes being renovated by expatriates and supervised by locals. Scaffolding props up crooked walls, enclosing dilapidated rooms filled with cranes and pulleys, masons, carpenters, old wooden beams, and centuries of dust.

By the eighth and final day, I had visited Jaouad in his salon to share some mint tea. He took a blow-dryer to my hair, styling it as straight and poofy as Catherine Deneuve's. To his delight, I had smoked fewer and fewer cigarettes each day. While I never saw Imad's masseuse, I was a bit more fit after the long climbs up and down *Talaa Kabira*. Ahmed and I enjoyed each other's company over dinner the last evening in a chic café in the *Ville Nouvelle*, the huge twenty-first-century city that surrounds the ancient medina. His friend Mohammed joined us, and he offered me a reliable ride back to Casablanca the next day.

I had given little Imane my small purple notebook in which she had written my name and hers in English. We were sitting together in the *dar's* courtyard on the last morning, counting to one hundred in as many languages as we could (skipping the numbers in each decade), while her mother—Imad's sister—tended to bed-and-breakfast business. Imane was happy to be six years old; my age was inconceivable to her and didn't matter anyway. We had learned the words for *girl* and *boy* in classic and Moroccan Arabic, French, and English.

I absorbed a lot and wrote a little. As the days cycled round, I listened to the muezzin in the minaret on the hill, coughing and clearing his throat before sounding the prayers that would be answered by others in mosques across the city. *Allah Akbar.* I understood his words: "God is great. Mohammed is his prophet."

As the trip drew to a close, the complacent turkey that stood quietly all week long in one of the medina's many poultry stalls had disappeared. It was time to go.

Having said good-bye to all, including the merchants I had come to know, I had chosen to spend the last few hours on my rooftop. I was unable to pull myself away from simply being.

My final lesson with Jaouad had ended with an Arab proverb: "It is better to know a thing than not to know it." We had wrestled with the language on the rooftop at dawn. We rearranged the diction, we parsed the meter, and we looked for the subtleties in translation. We finally found the poetry, its resonance revealed once we had simplified the expression to its bare bones.

EPILOGUE

Whenever it is a damp, drizzly November in my soul; whenever I find myself involuntarily pausing before coffin warehouses, and bringing up the rear of every funeral I meet; and especially whenever my hypos get such an upper hand of me, that it requires a strong moral principle to prevent me from deliberately stepping into the street, and methodically knocking people's hats off—then, I account it high time to get to sea as soon as I can.

—Herman Melville, *Moby Dick*

In March 2011, I decided to return to Marrakech. I was looking toward the following November, the November of Ishmael's restless soul, the beginning of crazed Western holidays that are treasured by so many but deplored by as many more, the time when daylight diminishes and winter darkness grows long. When the November rains set in and my office light begins to glow in the premature blackness, my spirit's longing starts to stir. November 2011 promised a space on my quotidian, drudge-worn calendar, days suddenly free of endless deadlines that might afford time to set sail.

Fes had captured my heart, but my sights were trained on Marrakech once more, to see it from as many perspectives as might be possible in ten precious, timeless days. And that is what I hoped to do, praying to Jesus, Allah, Moses, Brahma, and Buddha to protect me as I boarded a plane and sailed through the skies, bound again for Morocco.

Since my last trip, I've noticed that Morocco has been surfacing in the news. While I am certainly more attentive to Moroccan references, increased media coverage signals something larger and more acute than my newfound personal awareness. It has been a restless spring and fall in Northern Africa and countries to the East.

In February 2011, we began hearing news of a populist revolution in Tunisia, orchestrated through the wonders of social networking and leading to demands for democratization in that country. I e-mailed my friend Samia in Tunis, who said that her friends and family were well but dedicated to ensuring a fairer system of government so that protestors had not died in vain.

In March 2011, my friends Frank and Sarah caught the last flight out of Cairo for foreigners being evacuated after Egyptians, consumed by the Northern African freedom fever, were demanding government reform by deposing their dictator. Frank's body was dying of ALS, but his spirit, oh, his spirit wanted to travel, to see once more the great architecture and art of world civilizations. With a guide in tow and Sarah's fearless energy, they managed to see Egypt one last time. Kind people along the way transported Frank around the great pyramids and across narrow pedestrian bridges. He smiles at the camera as he squints at the sun from his wheelchair. It is worth the effort. A year later, his ashes fill an Egyptian amphora of translucent golden alabaster.

In late April 2011, someone in Morocco detonated a bomb that killed fifteen people gathered in a tourist café in Marrakech's famous *Djemma el-Fna*, the main square. A one-inch column buried in the newspaper bore the news without detail. A week later, US forces killed Osama bin Laden in Abbottabad, Pakistan. By July, Southern Sudan had declared its independence after a war that had slaughtered several million, an inconceivable number that rocks the mind—all that bloodshed and lives stolen—giving birth to the world's youngest nation. These events may or may not be related. I for one know too little to write about them. The *I* is rendered completely ignorant and insignificant, and writing becomes as choppy and violent as the subjects at hand. Ours is a restless world of discontent that carries us forward on incessant mantras of hope and despair. Killing and thriving, war and peace, feast and famine beat to the rhythms of the universe, catching us up in a relentlessly indifferent song.

Buddhists speak of equanimity—accepting the bad with the good, the dark with the light, the sad with the joyful, the loss with the gain. But so often the horror eclipses the beautiful, and we are simply overwhelmed. Yet as we struggle to reestablish the balance over and over again, reciting our prayers and meditations and seeking small daily miracles, we define our humanity.

By late June 2011, "Arab Spring" had become the journalistic title for the historic events of February 20, 2011, the democratic demands and antiregime protests that began in Tunisia and swept through Egypt. On July 1, 2011, Morocco held a referendum that was passed by 98 percent of those who voted. On the eve of the referendum, I heard an interview with a radio journalist in Rabat. In the days that followed, there were no further reports, as is so often the case with the ebb and flow of news features.

Instant messaging shrinks the globe, and yet the news we receive is still as sporadic as that in letters sent by ancient ships over the course of months. Even among those closest to us, our messages sometimes fail to reach each other. Clouds of selfishness and self-absorption obscure communication. Still, breakthroughs to clarity arise now and then. For me, the underlying, unquenchable desire to travel—a yearning to set sail into the unknown—provides the clarifying antidote to whatever hypos hound at home.

The reforms were seen as King Mohammed VI's efforts to move his country slowly and peacefully toward democracy, or rather a more equitable constitutional monarchy. Some interpreted the move as a new model for the "Arab Spring," a nonviolent response to revolutionary demands. Moroccans who boycotted the vote thought it merely a veiled attempt to appease the protests but retain the power. Idealists saw it as a new beginning, a phrase that seems redundant except that it embraces the realities of eternal cycles.

Continuing the reforms promised by the king in 1999, the 2011 referendum may have been a fresh attempt to avoid the upheavals of February 20 that led to the Tunisian and Egyptian revolutions, currently wracking Syria, Bahrain, and Yemen and bringing war to Libya, where my Arabic teacher was born. Educated in Egypt and now living in the States, she added our morning tutorials to her busy schedule of teaching at a local university. She sees good in the world and in her Islamic faith, but she is troubled by the fear and misunderstanding that news headlines often instill. She is devoted to education and community discussions that promote trust, helping to open hearts and minds.

And what of Morocco's reforms invited by the referendum? The significance of the proffered changes seemed to turn heads indeed. Perhaps not strides big enough for the extremes of Moroccan society or for a follow-up report by US broadcast news but measurable steps for a country that has been ruled by Mohammed VI's family for three centuries.

Morocco's constitution states that the king is sacred. That language will now be expunged. Berber, the country's indigenous tongue, will be acknowledged as the national language along with Arabic. The judicial system will be given greater authority, and government control will cede to the prime minister—appointed by the king, but chosen from the ruling party in parliament. The king retains power over defense, security, and the Islamic religious establishment as the *Amir al Mu'minin*, the commander of the faithful. A newspaper photo showed the queen, a computer scientist from Fes, casting her vote for the referendum while others in the background watched and waited.

And I too watch and wait. The prospects of a November journey were dimmed by the realities of work life. Indeed, relinquishing resistance and learning to accept the way things are help to counter disappointments in a Buddhist sort of way.

Aftershocks of the Arab Spring rocked the world. On October 20, 2011, Libyan forces captured and killed Muammar Gaddafi. Just days later, Tunisia held its first elections. In Egypt, protestors were gathering against the military. In December, American troops left Iraq as the United States declared an end to the nine-year war.

As I let go of the possibility of November 2011 travels, I looked toward the approach of the anniversary of the Arab Spring—February 20, 2012. Morocco shimmered on a very distant horizon, but it was only a mirage giving way to other conditions as they arose. In the meantime, as if by divine providence, my museum installed a work by Philadelphia artist Tristin Lowe—*Mocha Dick*, a fifty-two-foot fabric facsimile of the white whale that terrified the South Pacific's Mocha Islands and inspired Melville's creation. While I obsessed about chasing my virtual whales, I actually had one right there to keep me company, helping me to resist knocking people's hats off until I could set sail. Spring came round; Morocco beckoned. I could answer only with two resignations: The first to free myself from soul-sucking employment for which I knew I should be grateful but simply wasn't any longer. The second, an outcome of the first, to soothe my restless spirit by having unshackled at least one foot to move one step closer to the liberation of travel. *Sooner or later, sooner or later, sooner or later,* I chanted.

Then September 2012 arrived. Libyan terrorists or angry mobs—who can say? Labels never truly define their subjects—killed Chris Stevens, ambassador and one of the Middle East's greatest proponents, a man with the language, cultural understanding, and long view who was best suited for the delicate diplomatic dance. Three associates, rumored to be US intelligence agents, also died. Moderate Libyan citizens regretted the violence. Tunisian intellectuals decried and despaired of the anti-Western protests in their country, which traversed the East past Pakistan. The protests, some say, were provoked by a stupid Islamophobic video that made its way across the Internet from the States. Medieval. Crusading. We ask, who is really the infidel? Eventually or immediately, depending on the accounts, the US government painstakingly uncovered a terrorist plot by al-Qaeda that once again caught the West off guard.

In late September, Mohammed VI addressed the UN General Assembly, positioning the Kingdom of Morocco internationally. He spoke of troubled spots and troubled people—the Western Sahara, Mali, Syrian refugees—and urged a nonmember status for Palestine at the UN as well as negotiations to establish a Palestinian state, with East Jerusalem as its capital, to live "side by side with Israel, in peace and security."

And now, November is here yet again. A car bomb incinerated prominent security and intelligence officials in Beirut, a speculated overflow from the brutal Syrian civil war. Egyptians are protesting President Morsi's recent autocratic power play.

Last night, twilight sent chilling rains. The sky turned a dusty purple as clouds filtered pink rays, then released a downpour that drenched and scattered late autumn leaves into puddled roads. Reflections from streetlights and headlights bounced across asphalt surfaces mottled with yellows, oranges, and reds. Another change in season enlivened by its own singular beauty, engulfed in darkness.

"The worst of prisons is the self-created one," a character in Fatima Mernissi's *Dreams of Trespass* observes. And so, my soul, we move slowly and patiently, harboring eternal hope that the pendulum will swing us forward to peaceful sands of ancient lands so that we might see them again. *Inshallah.*

SELECT BIBLIOGRAPHY

Abouzeid, Leila. *Year of the Elephant: A Moroccan Woman's Journey toward Independence.* Translated by Barbara Parmenter. Austin, 1989.

Canetti, Elias. *The Voices of Marrakesh.* Translated by J. A. Underwood. London, 1967.

Coelho, Paolo. *The Alchemist.* Translated by Alan B. Clarke. New York, 1993.

Clarke, Suzanna. *A House in Fez: Building a Life in the Ancient Heart of Morocco.* New York, 2007.

Essaydi, Lalla. *Les Femmes du Maroc.* Essay by Fatima Mernissi. Brooklyn, 2009.

Lalami, Laila. *Hope and Other Dangerous Pursuits.* Orlando, 2005.

Lalami, Laila. *Secret Son.* New York, 2009.

Melville, Herman. *Moby Dick.* New York, 2003.

Mernissi, Fatima. *Dreams of Trespass: Tales of a Harem Girlhood.* New York, 1994.

Said, Edward S. *Orientalism.* New York, 1979.

Shah, Tahir. *In Arabian Nights: A Caravan of Moroccan Dreams.* New York, 2008.

Shah, Tahir. *The Caliph's House: A Year in Casablanca.* New York, 2006.

Wharton, Edith. *In Morocco.* NP, 2012.

CPSIA information can be obtained at www.ICGtesting.com
Printed in the USA
LVOW11s1519210914

405128LV00001B/293/P